# Heal Your Brokenness

## 10 powerful days that will change your life

## By  Christy Rutherford

*I dedicate this book and my life to God. Thank you for creating in me a clean heart. With you, all things are possible.*

*My family for loving me unconditionally.*

*All the leaders at Organo Gold. You've had an immense impact on my life.*

*E.S., for seeing the spiritual being in me until I saw her in myself. Forever grateful.*

# Table of Contents

# *Foreword*

Christy Rutherford is a leader of leaders, in every sense of the word. I first met Christy less than one year ago, at the event of one of our mutual heroes, Sharon Lechter (author of multiple best-seller books including "Think and Grow Rich for Women"). We became fast friends, and the common ground of our interests has grown substantially since then.

Christy is a stellar example of positive living and thinking. Her posts, her notes and her articles take the higher road and inspire others to a degree that when she occasionally takes a hard line stand in public, it is only after careful deliberations on the sensitivities of the people she addresses—all of them—with the words that she says. That topic, in fact, became the theme of an article I wrote with and about Christy as one of my Entrepreneur Channel pieces for Forbes.

In the realm of executive leaders, Christy is a breath of fresh air. While some experts take great pains to exude the loftiness of their positions, Christy is unaffected. Her happiness and natural sense of completeness is not only evident, but infectious. She is a living example of the principles she teaches, to a degree that no self-consciousness about the gravitas of her image is required.

Clearly, Christy is well acquainted with the principles that she teaches. In her earlier 2016 book "Shackled to Success" she outlines the life path that led her to a soaring career, a high salary and material possessions. On that path, she experienced constant physical pain. Debilitated to the point that she almost required a wheelchair, she came to recognize the pain was of her own making, in a life that was filled with "toxins" such as terrible leaders, a negative work environment, and undigested anger that was literally eating her body and spirit alive.

In "Shackled," she traced the path that allowed her to break away from the "safety" of her six-figure income to follow her personal dreams. She has learned to recognize her challenges as blessings.

In "Heal Your Brokenness," Christy offers a step-by-step guidebook for the way others can recognize their sticking points, large or small, heal in the areas needed, and embark upon a very *specific* plan for success. In every chapter, Christy offers her personal experience and wisdom in a format that is immediately useful to others. Each chapter produces wisdom with the simplicity and breadth of a Jim Rohn, offered up in a lesson format that allows readers to convert their learning to immediate action at every step of the way.

"Heal Your Brokenness" is a book that is interesting in its entirety, but also meant to be digested in pieces. Over a period of time, readers should take the opportunity to digest every morsel, perhaps covering a chapter a week and using notes or reminders to practice each new principle day by day as they go.

Christy's characteristic humor is present throughout her writing ("Spiritual development can't be microwaved"). You will come away from every chapter feeling as if you've just experienced a personal conversation with a trusted and personal friend. This is a book that I will treasure for many seasons to come.

Cheryl Snapp Conner
Founder of SnappConner PR, creator of Content University™
National columnist for Forbes.com, PC Magazine and guest contributor to the Wall Street Journal
Author of Forbes eBook *Beyond PR: Communicate Like a Champ in the Digital Age*
Named one of the world's Top 20 Business Thought Leaders to follow by Clearpoint Strategies in 2015.

# *Preface*

Over four years ago, I had everything that I wanted and nothing that I needed. I had a successful six-figure career, national achievements, my dream car, a nice place filled with nice things and expensive artwork, and I traveled at least twice a month.

By society's standard of S-U-C-C-E-S-S, I had it all. However, with everything I had and all I achieved, I was a walking pin cushion with a hardened heart. My inner light that once shined as a beacon, bringing cheer and goodwill to all I encountered, faded and only glimmered on occasion.

My inner spirit was stirring around and wanted to break out of the walls that I placed around myself to protect me from the world that had put a whooping on me. There was a battle going on for my soul. The Lord of Light and the entity of darkness were both vying for my attention, and I came to a crossroads where I had to make a choice.

I looked good, smelled good and smiled, but all of that was a lie. It was a lie and I was an actress who deserved an Academy Award for pretending to be happy, while my soul howled to be turned loose and take precedence in my life again. I had so much inner turmoil and stress from my job, that I thought I was going to die. I chose the Lord of Light and resigned from my successful career and jumped off a cliff with blind faith that I would be okay. When I got out of the fire and away from people who were sucking the oxygen out of me, I was able get a glimpse of how I created the negative environment I found myself in.

I discovered that regardless of how much I worked, how many books I read and audiobooks listened to, there was a wooing of my soul and spirit. They were calling me to reconnect on another level. God was calling me to BECOME who I was always meant to be in this world in order to serve others. I saw the vision long ago, but got off track when I steered my career in a different direction.

The path was already laid out and the script was written, but I had to get back on the path and move towards my destiny. This process has been absolutely excruciating, yet exhilarating in rediscovering the person I buried long ago. She was buried behind walls that were guarded by vicious dogs, a 30 foot high barbed wire fence, and under a pile of broken bricks that once housed my reality. I had to dig her up and get busy!

There was someone I was meant to BECOME and a way that I wanted to FEEL. Hmmmm...a feeling. I was searching for the feeling that seemed elusive and the one that I thought high levels of success would bring. After achieving success and not feeling the way I thought it would feel, I was searching for another feeling...**wholeness**. What does it FEEL like? Well, I wasn't exactly sure, but I knew that I would know it when I felt it again.

Although I was working on several entrepreneurial projects, I wasn't chasing success, money or material possessions anymore. I was chasing wholeness. I've had success and all those other qualities already, but realized I created some holes and blind spots in my life. I wanted to be whole again, not broken.

Creating new habits and changing as an adult is tough, but absolutely possible. I vowed to put just as much relentless effort and pursuit into successfully BECOMING who I was meant to be and FEELING the way I wanted to feel, just as I had done in my career. I was willing to do whatever it took until I discovered it.

Honestly, I didn't know how broken I was until I met whole people. I didn't know how much toxicity and stress I carried until I no longer worked in an environment that created it. I didn't know how unhealthy I had become until I became healthy again.

Back pain, neck pain, and headaches had become a normal part of my life and I had gotten used to being in "general pain," so it didn't set off any red flags to me. There are plenty of medications targeting specific pains, so surely, this is a common issue that many people face. I was completely unaware that pain is not normal and I had the power to change it, but only if I was willing to change myself.

My life wasn't going to change until I decided to do something different and go after what I wanted in blind and relentless faith knowing that one day I would find what I was looking for. I have found the feeling and wish to share the insight with you.

## The Sequel

This is the second book in a series intended to bring light into the lives of people who are living in darkness. The first book, *Shackled To Success*, exposed my vulnerabilities, bad habits and the dark place I found myself in.

Writing it was a painful and excruciating experience. Why? Because I had to dig up skeletons that I had not seen in a long time. I closed the door on that entire period of my life and no longer acknowledged it existed. Digging around in that closet was no longer serving me and telling the stories for the sake of complaining didn't sit well with me, so I closed the door on that portion of my life, locked it and walked away.

Standing in the perspective of who I AM today, I knew that I had to go back into the closet and share the lessons learned and save others from toxic circumstances. Opening that closet and revisiting my past shocked and unsettled me. I COULD NOT BELIEVE that I secretly lived in that much pain for that long. I couldn't believe that I lost the close connection with my family for that long. I couldn't believe that not forgiving others and being resentful created dysfunctions in my relationships and friendships.

Standing in who I AM today gives me the perspective and insight to assist others that are in pain and searching for a way out of it. My goal is to share practical and useful information to assist you with creating the life that you truly desire. That's my Purpose in life and is what I have been called to do. To use my pain, my lessons and what I learned to serve others and pull them out of the darkness and into the light. To be strong enough to share my vulnerabilities in an effort to serve you.

## Broken Past Or New Future?

Which is easier, trying to glue together pieces of a broken vase or using a potter's wheel to create a new one? One involves headaches and frustration to get tiny pieces to fit together, knowing it will never be whole again. The other is new and exciting, even with its imperfections, until the finished work is revealed. What are you choosing for a broken life?

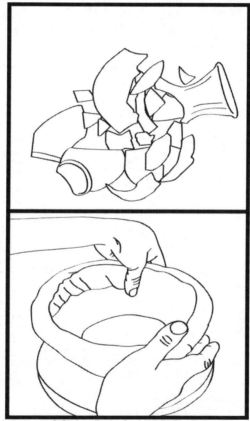

## Hitting Reset

I hit the RESET button on my life and have spent the past four years recreating, reshaping and molding the life that I dreamed about long, long ago. I've invested over $140,000 in events, camps and programs in order to create Christy 2.0. I've read countless books and listened to thousands of hours of audios and studied with some of the world's greatest leaders.

At a conference nearly three years ago, I worked to discover my Purpose in life and what I'm supposed to accomplish while I'm here on this earth, in this lifetime. After digging and digging and uncovering, this is what I wrote,

*"My mission is to illuminate the light in millions of people around the world by coaching and nurturing their inner spirits and egos. To restore people back to their authentic selves, thereby allowing them to experience health and mental wellness, balance in life and work, and financial prosperity."*

One separate poster, I drew my future life and at the top titled it with a quote, "Be the change I want to see in the world." Ghandi said, "Be the change you want to see in the world." I changed that quote to speak to my inner spirit. I was speaking a secret code to myself that I needed to BECOME the mission statement, before I was able to teach it to others.

I hung this over my bed and read it every night and during the day. I was so far away from being this person and she was only a figment of my imagination, a secret desire, but I knew she was really there. Unearthing spiritual greatness has been my full time job and has been both elevating and deflating. It has been filled with tremendous triumphs and devastating breakings.

By uncovering, unraveling and unearthing the dreams that I buried, I have found the feeling of wholeness. By regaining my spirit, my dignity, my character, I have found the feeling of wholeness. By reconnecting with my family and discovering who my real friends are, I have found the feeling of wholeness.

It's my hope that sharing how I got this feeling of unexplainable peace, bliss and happiness, that you will apply the lessons to shortcut your path to happiness, and find the feeling you've been searching for. Let's walk together and work together to Heal Your Brokenness and get you on the path to living your life in wholeness.

# Chapter 1

# *The Process*

*"A lot of people have a gift that will take them somewhere, but not enough character to keep them there once they get there."*
*- Joyce Meyer*

This book reveals 10 lessons that if learned and applied, they will absolutely change your life! However, you have to actually take action on what I'm recommending and not simply think you can get the results through osmosis. I can tell you that some of the recommendations will make you uncomfortable and may seem unrealistic, but in a world where misery and unhappiness is normal and expected, it's time to go against the grain to get what you desire.

I have been reading self-help magazines and books since I was 12 years old. I would read fitness magazines and books while eating chips and cookies. I just like to read random information on how to solve issues and often gave people advice based on something that I read. I applied some of the information, but as a leader, I used it for other people.

It wasn't until I took a break from assisting other people and actually started to apply the information in my own life, that I experienced significant change. I knew what needed to be done, but it was easier to read it and tell others what to do than to apply it in my own life.

Once I started applying the information fervently and actually started to see and feel the results, I applied more and more. There are hundreds of lessons to share, but I'm sharing 10 that will make significant impacts in your life today.

## 5 Stages

There are five stages/processes in each of the lessons you will learn in this book.

1. Reading
2. Understanding
3. Applying
4. Seeing change
5. Pedal to the medal

*Reading* - First, read the book all the way through. Some of the information will resonate with you as an immediate pain point and some may not relate to you at all. Now that you know that happiness and joy can be a reality for you if you actually take action, imagine yourself FEELING the way you want to feel.

*Understanding* - Secondly, after reading the book, go back to the lesson that you felt the greatest pain for and the issues that you may be struggling with. I suggest that you work on that issue first, because solving the biggest issue first, may resolve several smaller issues.

*Applying* – Noting the way that you want to feel, consciously apply the information and track your progress. Buy a journal specifically for this book and take notes on how you felt the first time you actually applied the information. Good, bad or indifferent.

1. How did you feel?
2. How did other people feel as a result of it?
3. How did you feel about how other people felt?
4. Too much? Too little?
    a. What can you do differently?

*Seeing Change* – What are the noted changes? Do you feel better, and do you feel like you have more space and oxygen? Once you dip your toe in the water and get a taste of the feeling, it will be time to go full throttle and put the...

*Pedal to the Medal* – If you want to accelerate your results, you can speed up the process and go all in. Going all in of course will cause greater shifts in your life and will seem dramatic and traumatic, but if you're at the point where you are going nuts, and you're looking for a way out of the hole you may be in, go all in. Change creates pain. Staying the same is painful. Choose your pain.

## Becoming Who?

Seven years ago, I wanted the peace of Eckhart Tolle; the desire for growth of Oprah; the wisdom of Dr. Maya Angelo and Dr. Wayne Dyer; and the freedom of Elizabeth Gilbert in *Eat, Pray, Love*.

As the years passed, I wanted to joy and lightness of Pastor Joel Osteen; to be able to speak into the soul of others like Bishop TD Jakes and Dr. Myles Munroe; the wit and funniness of Pastor John Gray and Jim Rohn. Also, the ability to tell stories like Joyce Meyer, and the success insight of Napoleon Hill and everyone he studied.

I wasn't exactly sure how all these qualities would fit into my body and spirit, but I wanted it anyway. I studied the leaders, read their writings and watched their speeches to get their foundational knowledge and philosophies.

Ahhh yes...philosophies. We are all unique individuals with specific missions while we are here in this lifetime, but there are success principles and philosophies that have been around for centuries.

Although I've made significant strides in my growth, am I perfect? Absolutely not! Am I a saint? Nope! Am I better that I used to be? Absolutely!

But still there wasn't clarity around whether or not I had BECOME who I wanted to be.

## Tests Prove Growth

Yes, yes, yes, all of this sounds good in theory and after significant growth and development, I was still nervous and wondered if it was really possible to become EXACTLY who I wanted to be. Was all the work, all the pain, the sacrifices and studying worth it? How would I know that I had become that magical and mystical person I secretly desired to be?

3

You don't know who you are and what you've learned until you are tested. More importantly, to recognize adversity as a test. I've learned there is a lesson in every negative scenario and it's meant to teach us something about ourselves and others. I'm always searching for the hidden meaning in situations that most people complain about.

How will you know that you've finally accepted your family member's dysfunction, when they once grated your nerves, if they don't actually grate your nerves, and you don't react like you used to? As you learn and apply this information, know that you will be tested. Sometimes you will feel like there has to be hidden cameras somewhere, because of the level of ridiculousness you may experience.

There were a few lessons that I went around and around and around on for months, until I finally saw the pattern and realized I needed to do something different to move to the next level. Changing your life doesn't eliminate adversities and challenges, but it will give you the perspective and ability to choose a different reaction; which ultimately changes the result.

## My Final Exam

Before writing this series of books, I was waiting for confirmation. But confirmation of what and how would I know I was ready? The only way I would know that my default and my "peel one layer back" Christy was totally annihilated, is if I was severely tested.

Earlier this year, I spent a time with two people I thought were my friends. The first one cursed me out several times and treated me in a way I didn't expect or appreciate. The situation was so petty, that it was almost comical. The first time she cursed me out, it was after I asked her if she wanted some sweet potato fries. She said, "Don't you ever tell anyone you brought that *&^% in my house!"

After giving her a blank stare, I shrugged my shoulders and said, "Okay, I guess that's a no." I know that hurting people hurt people, and I don't allow them to inflict their pain on me. Sweet potato fries were considered appalling to someone who considers themselves healthy, but what goes into your mouth does not make you unclean. It's what comes out of your mouth, because what comes out of your mouth comes out of your heart. There was no need for me to react to that.

She talked to me sideways for a few days and some of the situations I found myself in, I started laughing and said, "Really God? You are just stacking them all up aren't you?"

*The test: Will I allow someone in pain to inflict their pain on me? Will I respond to negativity with increased negativity and hurt people who hurt me?*

The next test came from another perceived friend who questioned my character and integrity, after getting the timelines of my journey mixed up in her head.

*The test: Will I allow someone's harsh and uninformed judgment of me change the way I feel about myself?*

If you had the opportunity to read *Shackled to Success*, you would know my reaction to people who offended me was similar to fried rice at a Hibachi grill. I would throw heat on you, light you up, and slice and dice you...all while eloquently adding curse words and other expletives to make the experience more colorful. Also, flipping the spatula in the air and tossing pans to the side. I was a furniture mover! LOL!

But, that's not who I am anymore and that's the person I was secretly afraid of. Was she still there hiding and lurking, waiting to be activated? These ladies met me after the growth, and didn't know about my history of using words as razor blades that would leave people bleeding long after I walked away.

I have become crystal clear on who I AM, where I'm going, and why I'm here, so anything counter to the vision I have of myself and my future doesn't affect me. If someone offers an image or criticism of me that's not in alignment with what I KNOW about myself, all the way to the cellular level, it doesn't affect me. How other people feel about me is none of my business. The only thing that matters is how I feel about myself and after nearly 40 years, I'm so madly in love with myself, that I won't let anyone become between us (me and the voice in my head).

Because of that, I'm proud to report that there was no furniture moving, no cursing, no one was injured and they both still have their dignities intact. I just gave both of them a blank stare and walked away with my peace. They actually ridiculed me, because they took my non-response as weakness.

What they don't realize is, not responding is a sign of strength, not weakness, because it shows that I'm no longer manipulated by the ignorance and short comings of other people. When you react to other people, you are usually reacting from a past pain point or baggage that you're carrying around. I don't have that issue anymore, but I wouldn't have known unless I was tested.

Although we aren't friends anymore, I have forgiven them and I'm actually grateful for what they did *for* me and not *to* me. Without the test, I wouldn't have known that what I'm sharing actually works. I thank them and wish them well in their future endeavors, health and happiness.

**Pinball Machine**
Using a pinball machine as an analogy, the past, stored pain and baggage represent the pegs that light up once they're hit with the pinball. The pinball is a person's negative ball of energy they throw at you when they criticize you or say something negative. When we respond and react to other people, the intensity of the response is based on how many pegs they connect with and the total score. If the score is less than 100, they'll get a mild response. If the score is over 10,000, the rage response that comes from you will make their teeth rattle in the back of their throat.

Can you relate to this photo?

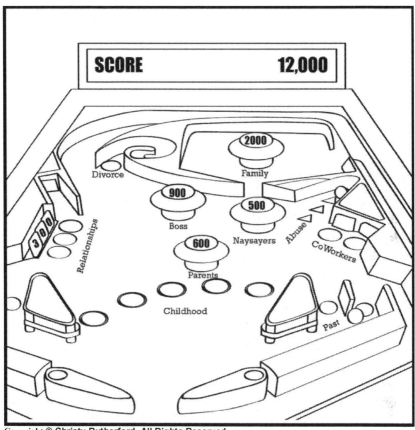

SCORE 12,000

If someone says something to you, what's lighting up in your body? What old situations are ringing in your ear, saying:

"Ding! My co-worker talked to me like that!"

"Ding! My father treated me like crap!"

"Ding! My ex-wife did the same thing!"

"Ding! My classmates picked on me!"

When you react to people, they are pulling your strings and manipulating you. This makes you a victim of outer circumstances and you feel like you're not in control of your life. I'm here to tell you that you are.

The Process

When you work to let go of your baggage, past hurts, and pain, and work toward forgiveness, you resolve your inner conflict. When you resolve your inner conflict, you won't be manipulated or controlled by outer circumstances.

*"If there's no enemy within, the enemy outside can do no harm."*
*- African Proverb*

Do the work! Choose to change your life for you and no one else. You are now holding the key that will allow to you become a better and greater version of yourself. I'm excited for your future. Let's get started!!

# Chapter 2

# *Admitting Unhappiness*

*"A man only begins to be a man when he ceases to whine and revile and commences to search for the hidden justice which regulates his life, and as he adapts his mind to that regulating factor, he ceases to accuse others as the cause of his condition, and builds himself up in strong and noble thoughts."*
*– James Allen*

While getting my Leadership Coaching certification from Georgetown Univ, we were taught a happiness scale. I can't remember the creator, but I remember the scale. There are plenty of scales that are used in doctor's offices that have smiley faces on them to depict the level of pain you're in or how you feel that day.

The happiness scale goes from (-3 to +3).

Based on the numbers, -3 is being in steaming frustrated, 0 is content and +3 is a euphoric happiness, similar to being high. They said that most people live at 0 or at +1 and are generally content with life, but they aren't amazing or euphorically happy.

I told a few of my classmates that I wanted live in a +3 and make that my normal. Why not? They said that it was unrealistic to aspire for such a state of mind. As an overachiever and someone who loves to go against the grain, I made it my mission to attain a +3 state of mind and make that my normal.

I started to monitor my feelings periodically throughout the day and measure where I was on the scale. If I was at a 0 or a -1 for an extended period, I had to determine what was creating the low energy and make tweaks to fix it and increase the numbers. This practice started in 2009 and over time, I became more in tune with how outside forces affected me internally.

Awareness is the first step. Taking action is the next. As time passed and after nearly 8 months of being in the negative, not even getting to 0, I resigned from my successful career. This was a HUGE step, but before the happiness scale, I walked around unaware of how I felt and how I wanted to feel.

The fact that I had a goal and a feeling to shoot for, made me aware consciously aware of how I felt most of the time. Either I would become content with knowingly being miserable, or I could take action to change it.

## +3 Is Child-Like Happiness

When people meet me, they note the abnormal amount of happiness that exudes from me. Living in a +3 is INCREDIBLE, but people think I'm weird, and that's okay. It's only annoying to people who have become content with being miserable. They often ask, "Why are you so happy?"

My first response is, "I woke up this morning in my right mind, with good health and can get out of the bed unassisted. Whatever happens after that is my choice. If I choose to have a fantastic day, then I will. If I choose to have stress, anxiety or depression, well, those conditions will be granted too."

At what point did having child-like happiness become abnormal? When did the desire to live in a +3 become unrealistic? Why is it more normal and acceptable to have anxiety, stress and depression and self-medicate to alleviate the issues, but not resolve them?

Using my little cousin as an example, she's three years old and hilarious. Her unbound joy and happiness lights up every room she enters. My family relishes in her freedom and courage to attempt new things. When she fails at doing something for the first time, we cheer for her and encourage her to keep trying until she's successful. When she finally gets it right, we cheer loudly and celebrate.

On the contrary, if she pouted and displayed unhappiness for an hour, similar to what's considered *normal* for adults, we would become concerned. If her lack of enthusiasm, moodiness, sadness and low energy continued for more than three days, we would take her to the doctor, because there's obviously something wrong.

When the doctor asks, "What's wrong with her?" We would report "She's unhappy, not playful and sad. Although she's eating well, she doesn't have a temperature. Even though she's not displaying signs of any acute illnesses, she's also not displaying signs of joy."

The doctor would run a series of tests and scans to try to find the root cause of her condition. What if he came back and said, "This child is perfectly healthy physically, but has early onset of the mental state of an adult?"

Now, ponder for a moment. At what point in our lives did it become okay for us to display the same emotions described above for years on end? In children, we would be greatly concerned, but fail to be concerned about ourselves.

## Unhappy During The Prime of Our Lives

A 2010 Economist article depicted a scale to show a "U-bend" of happiness, based on age. According to the graph, our happiness levels peak at 18 years old, and then decline *sharply* in our early 20's. It starts to level out and then dips again in our late 30s. Then, increases again mid-50s, and peak in our mid-60's. According to this graph, most people reach the point of happiness that was experienced in our first 18 years of life again in our mid-60's.

Looking at the age range where people aren't happy, it's during the time we are considered adults and usually enter the workforce. One would assume that as we rush to enter the workforce, eager to make our mark on the world and climb the corporate ladder, that we would be happier. However, the statistics (and real life examples) show otherwise.

The majority of us spend the peak of our lives at the lowest point of happiness, only to realize as we become more mature (dare I say older) that we need to make the rest of our lives, the best of our lives.

Why is the happiness of an 18-year-old regained at the age of 65? Is this the point where we realize we have fewer days in front of us than behind us? Can it be attributed to seeing close friends and family pass away due to old age or sudden illness?

It should be considered lunacy to continue to be stuck in the rat race and not find your way out until you are in your 60's. Why not live your best life for the majority of your life and not succumb to being a normal and content adult?

Well......there's a problem with that. Actually, there are a LOT of problems. However, we don't have as many problems as we have decisions to make. Indecision causes unhappiness, which causes stress, anxiety and depression. Stress creates all sorts of health issues.

Happiness and living a life with less stress and anxiety starts with a DECISION. I have found that it takes just as much effort to be miserable as it does to be happy. If you want things to change, you must be willing to change.

### More Money = More Happiness?

Have you ever seen rich people that were unhappy? Have you seen poor people that were happy? If rich people can be unhappy with money, and poor people can be happy without it, is happiness really about money. I can honestly say that some of my family members who don't make over $30,000 a year were happier than I was when I made $100,000. They were also in better health, because the prolonged and unmanaged stress from my career was ravaging my body into disease and decay.

Expanded roles and responsibilities at work command a higher salary, but it also comes with more stress. A 2010 study by Princeton revealed emotional well-being rose along with income up to $75,000, but there was no further progress of emotional well-being above that income level.

My friends and I laugh all the time about how we were happier at $45,000 than we were/are at $100,000+. Now, don't get me wrong, I'm not advocating against achieving high levels of income, but it's about realizing what's given up along the way from $45,000 to $100,000. Acknowledging that we lost "something" as we gained more income, credibility, job titles and reputations in our chosen profession, is the key to being happy with more money. What were we doing at $45,000 that we aren't doing at $100,000?

At $45,000, we were fresh out of college and super proud of the accomplishment of getting our first job. We were happy with moving into our very own apartment, typically furnished with hand-me down furniture or pieces from discount stores. We were happy with our used cars.

The freedom and excitement of accomplishments were celebrated often and we gathered regularly with friends for dinner, movies and birthday parties; often seeing each other several days a week outside of work or at least twice a month for dinner where we could get a great meal for $15.

We had responsibility, but it wasn't a ton, because we were young and the expectations and penalties for mistakes weren't as crushing.

Over time, as we ascended up the ladder of achievement, work became a priority and accomplishments became a normal part of life; so they were no longer celebrated. With additional income, our apartments turned into houses with mortgages and our used cars were replaced with new ones. Stress and anxiety from working longer hours accompanied the higher income.

Money that was once considered disposable income for gatherings with friends, is now being used for nicer homes, cars, furniture and other material possessions. Our $15 dinners turned into $50. People got married and had kids and the once close relationships with others aren't so close anymore. The attention has to be in the home and at work.

Friends who had kids and became stay at home moms developed depression, because their professional identity was replaced with picking up dirty socks and becoming a pseudo cab driver to kid's activities.

Now here we are in these big houses, driving these cars and have several post-graduate degrees, but we are also stressed out and over-worked in high level positions. We have anxiety and strained relationships with family and friends because Father Time waits for no one, and the weekly/monthly gatherings have turned into once every few years, if ever.

As we try to balance work, stress, family, spouses, care-giver or whatever role we are called to do, there are questions raised on whether or not it's worth it. Achieving executive level positions and breaking barriers is exciting, and a lofty goal to achieve. However, what happens when we get there and look at all that was lost along the way?

While we ascend to high positions, no one highlights the trade-off. There is an exchange taking place. More money, less time; more time, less money; bigger house, less disposable income; more disposable income, smaller house or apartment.

## Are You Unhappy?

How are you spending the best part of your life? At some point or another in our lives, it's likely we have shifted personalities to match the situation we're in or the circle that we associate with. It's a natural part of life to grow and evolve, but who are you evolving into?

Have you become someone who's kind and loving? Have you become someone who's stressed, short tempered, or angry? Have you sunk into depression? Have you developed a beautiful soul or are you bitter? Are you becoming the childhood neighbor you loved, or the one you ran away from?

Knowing where you are today, and observing where you want to be, you can make a DECISION to change your attitude and behavior. It's absolutely possible to live a life of happiness and joy, free from stress, anxiety and depression.

If you want your life to change, then you must start with the man/woman in the mirror. In order to get to the next destination, it's important to assess where you are today and go from there.

Here's an easy self-assessment to help identify your starting point.

### Are you a Happiness Fairy?
- Upon waking up, do you smile and are happy to be alive? (Happiness Fairies know waking up is not guaranteed, so it's a delight.)
- Is your goal to bring joy to others?
- Do you find joy in the small things?
- Do you take baked goods to the office?
- When others see you coming, do they light up and smile?
- Do you laugh more than 10 times a day?
- Do people ask you constantly, "Why are you so happy?"

### Are you Debbie Downer?
- Do you complain ALLLL day?
- Can you find joy in anything?
- When you awake in the morning, are you grateful for waking up or feel overwhelmed with the tasks of the day?
- Are you constantly waiting for the next tragedy in your life?
- Is this a common phrase? "….story of my life!"
- Does a dark cloud follow you everywhere you go?
- When you are walking towards others, do they frown or look down?
- Do people rush you off the phone or don't answer when you call?
- Do you suffer from depression?

### *Are you Groucho?*
- Do you snap at people before and after your coffee?
- If you looked in the mirror, are your eyebrows furled?
  - o Is that look normal? (unibrows don't count)
- Does everyone piss you off?
- When you walk towards others, do they move or go the other way?
- Do you have constant headaches and tightness in your chest?
- Do you have high levels of stress and anxiety?
- Do you use the word "hate" a lot?
  - o I hate this car.
  - o I hate my boss.
  - o I hate him/her.

Which one of the three personality types are you at this season of your life? At this moment, you have the CHOICE to choose which one you want to be tomorrow. I think we all want to be happy (even if secretly), but sometimes the yellow brick road to happiness looks like a mine field covered with rocks, booby traps and past hurts, and it's a looooooong road back. If you choose to blow the dust off of the road and navigate your way back on the path, it's well worth the journey.

## Guarding Yourself Against People In Pain
It took a long time for me to learn that we can't control other people. You can only control yourself and your reaction to them. Who are you surrounding yourself with and how easy can they set you off? Do you let strangers ruin your day?

If you're in a good mood, do you allow Debbie D to spew negativity all over you and then feel like crap for having interacted with him/her? If Groucho snaps at you, do you relive that moment all day and then become a Debbie D by telling others, and ruin their day? Do you allow others to trigger your pain points and then relive the saga of a past experience? It's a cycle. You can't stop others from snapping or complaining, but you can guard yourself against them.

I discussed these characters with one of my clients and shared how we unknowingly allow others to manipulate our feelings. He used the insight to manage himself with someone who brought up an incident that was a known pain point for him. The person couldn't understand why was he walking around happy all the time, when he should have still been pissed off for what his boss did to him the year before. *Isn't it funny how other people tell us how we should feel about something and then drag us back down to misery?*

My client said he felt stress and anxiety entering his body, and his head tightened from thinking about the incident. He then recalled our conversation and said to himself, "If I engage this guy in conversation, I'm going to be pissed off. Then, I'm going to drive home mad (road rage), have a drink, likely snap at my wife and won't be mentally present for my kids. Nope! I'm not going to let him do that to me." He told the guy, "Hey, I'm good and actually, I have to go." S-U-C-C-E-S-S!!

Being attentive to how you feel and how others make you feel takes practice, but it's worth it. My client is happier now than he's been in over 15 years.

**Distance Yourself From Negative People**

Practice blowing people off that make you feel like crap. If you are working on getting your happiness and peace back, talking to frazzled people constantly will delay the process. If you're ready for a change, then you need to make yourself a priority and start working to break the cycle of things you're doing that are no longer in alignment with your personal goals. Will you be brave enough to take your life back?

Have you ever seen someone's name on your caller ID and instantly stopped breathing, felt stressed, got a headache and/or your heart raced? Your body is trying to tell you something. Are you listening? DO NOT ANSWER IT! Even if it's a family member.

Conversations with people like that are best handled over text or email. Write them and say, "Pretty busy, what can I do for you?" If they say they wanted to tell you about their day, say you will call them back when you get a chance and just never get that chance. They are looking to dump on someone and don't let it be you. They will run through the rolodex of their phone until they find someone to share their negativity with. Save yourself!!

If you have to answer it, turn the volume down on the phone so you don't hear them. They don't care if you are listening, they just want to vent. I like to take my phone off of speakerphone and all I hear is whomp whomp whomp. After two to three minutes, I politely get off the phone.

Some may say that this is self-serving and we should to listen to others when they are in need. Well...I've talked to enough people in my lifetime to know that there are people who talk about their problems all day and there are others who are taking action to solve theirs. You can't do them both at the same time. While you are listening to others talk about their problems, you are missing valuable time that can be used to solve yours. We only have 24 hours in a day, how are you using yours

# Small Tweaks – Big Results
# Happiness

People think that it takes a huge change to be happy. As discussed earlier, huge shifts can cause greater results, but can also cause greater trauma. Either you are going to slowly peel off the Band-Aid or rip it off. Both are painful. Ripping it off is more painful, but the pain doesn't last as long.

The rate at which you implement these recommendations will be based on your personal experience and desires. Also your level of how fed up you are with your current circumstances. If you are mildly uncomfortable, you won't be in a hurry to make huge changes. If you are sick and tired of being sick and tired, then you'll go faster.

## Action Steps

**1. Assess Where You Are** – You can't figure out where you're going without knowing where you are. Please be honest with yourself.

    a) On the happiness scale, -3 to +3, where are you right now?

    b) What are the number of days you're in the negative?

    c) Are you as happy as you would like to be?

    d) Which character are you? If you don't know, ask someone in the office that doesn't really like you. They won't spare your feelings.

**2. What Will Make You Happy?** - Determine exactly what will make you happy, without thinking about how others would feel about it. What will make YOU happy? Many times we feel like we would hurt others if we really did what we wanted to do (ethically of course), but we live our lives as a slave to making others happy and then blame them for our unhappiness. That stops TODAY! You are solely responsible for your happiness. What will make YOU happy?

**3. Determine Your Sweet Spot** – Your sweet spot is doing what you want to do unapologetically. We have buried what we really want to do in life to appease others and to be liked by everyone. We want to be realistic. What do you secretly long to do, but think it's unrealistic and you're not sure others would agree? That's your sweet spot.

**4. Monitor Yourself Around Other People** - Be mindful of whether or not a conversation with others make you feel better or worse. Make a mental note and write their names down. Then, create a plan for managing yourself when you are around them.

| Action | Date | Notes |
|---|---|---|
| Read | | |
| Understand | | |
| Apply | | |
| See Change | | |
| Pedal to the Medal | | |

If you need more clarity on where you are and the areas that you may want to touch on in your life, go to www.christyrutherford.com/balance and get my free Work-Life Balance assessment. It will highlight areas that you may not be considering while determining your overall happiness.

# Chapter 3

# *Take Ownership Of Your Circumstances*

*"The Strangest Secret in the world is…you become what you think about most of the time."*
*- Earl Nightengale*

A few years ago, while traveling on a rental car shuttle to an airport, I engaged two gentlemen in conversation. I love to talk to other people, but was disappointed when the conversation turned negative. One of them excitingly spoke of being a 42-year-old boxer wanting to make a comeback. He then put his head down and told the story of what happened to him 20 years ago that stopped him from getting back in the ring. He sunk low in his seat, exhaled and gazed out of the window in a state of mild depression.

I've learned not to engage others in negative conversations. After he said that he was trying to "make a comeback," I quickly became busy on my phone checking emails and hoped to disappear into the seat, but that didn't work.

Now pseudo depressed himself from the details of the would-be boxer's tragic story, the other gentleman looked at me, deeply exhaled and then asked, "So….what's your story?"

"I don't have a story," I said.

"Everyone has a story."

"You mean the story I tell myself over and over again that keeps me from living the life I want? I'm sorry, I don't have one of those."

"There has to be something. No one has a perfect life."

"Yes, we all have a story, I have decided to use positive stories to empower me and not live in the negative ones."

My uncommon response stunned both of them, but it was my choice as to whether or not I would join their pity party, and I chose not to. Remember the story from the previous chapter that hurting people hurt people? I chose not to allow others to create stress and anxiety in my life as I was celebrating a beautiful day.

How many times do we allow others to engage us and ruin a great day by touching the unresolved pain points we carry? This line of thinking took discipline, practice, and steady application until it became my new normal. There was a turning point where I chose to become responsible for my life, feelings, and how I allowed others to make me feel.

Once I took control of my mind, (one few things we were given at birth) the sad, depressing and negative stories went away. I was able to eliminate stress and anxiety from my life, simply by focusing on becoming a better version of myself and not paying attention to how other people live their lives.

## Law of Attraction

I'm almost embarrassed to admit that I used to go to psychics in the various cities I lived in. I needed them to tell me what my future looked like. Would my life always be amazing professionally and suck personally? Would I ever get married and have kids or would I be the lady with 50 cats? What does my future hold?

One thing I've learned that's as absolute as the Law of Gravity, is that the Law of Attraction works whether or not you know it exists. The Law of Attraction was popularized with the book and DVD, *The Secret* by Rhonda Byrnes, but has been around for centuries.

After going around and around in life and seeking advice from others about how long I would live an undesired personal life, I learned that *I controlled my future*. I had been riding in the passenger side of my life's car, and needed to take the wheel and steer it in the direction that I wanted.

Six years ago, I started focusing on what I wanted my total life to look like and it was significantly different than the life I was living at the time. After getting clear on what I wanted my future life to look like, this is what I repeated to myself:

*"When I retire, I want my office to be outside. I want to be of greater service to people in need. I want to have less stress. I want teach people how to manage their stress. I want to be closer with my family. I want to create deeper relationships. I want to be a blessing to others and I want to be a beacon of shining light in a dark world."*

What I wanted wasn't based on money, material possessions or high levels of success. I had those already. I wanted something different than what I had worked for and created over a 16-year career. I am now living the exact life that I imagined, but better yet, I feel the way I wanted to feel. Living the life that I desired took great courage, sacrifice and a lot of dissolved friendships, but it was worth it.

Taking control of your life and CREATING your circumstances, (rather than being run by them) takes awareness and discipline. The exercise in the previous chapter should have offered clarity on where you are right now and where you want to be. Now, let's look at how to get there.

The Law of Attraction, means you get what you focus on most of the time. Take a moment to think about what you focus on most of the time. Think about it.

For the most part, we spend majority of our time trying to piece together a broken past. Wondering what shoulda, woulda, coulda, only if we had done something different. We hold on to the pain of past relationships and then carry that baggage and toxicity into our next one. We focus on all the qualities that we don't want in a mate and somehow ONLY attract that person in our life.

There are no new problems or scenarios in life and every issue that you have, someone has conquered and wrote about it. There are a gazillion videos on YouTube, but we spend our time watching a cat roller skate or a dancing baby. We don't use that same time to take advantage of personal development or spiritual videos that feature some of the world's greatest leaders. Again, we all have 24 hours in a day. How are you spending your time?

## Staying Miserable Is A Choice

In my previous career, I mentored over 70 people. When some of them felt trapped in their career, I advised them to create a Plan B by getting clarity on what they wanted their future to look like. Also, to save their money, and get the necessary credentials for what they wanted to do next. That way, they could survive if the job folded, or could leave when they wanted to.

When you don't have a Plan B, the thought of losing a job creates anxiety. Even worse, the thought of *leaving* a job creates fear, stress, anxiety and depression. Many people call it Golden Handcuffs, which is a self-created condition.

One young lady I mentored spoke of how she was miserable in her position. She didn't like her boss, felt undervalued and was falling into depression. I advised that if she was so stressed out and unhappy, instead of complaining, she should make a DECISION and submit her resignation letter.

Instead of taking ACTION, she fumbled with reasons, blamed other people for her woes and then called back the following week with more drama. Same story line, but a different set of characters.

She was suffocating in a cage that was created in her own mind. Her stress, anxiety and depression came from not having a Plan B or being clear on what she wanted her life to look like. She was living in the expectations of others, but wasn't clear on what she wanted.

I advised her to continue to give her best effort at work and turn off the television, get off the couch and get a Master's degree in the career field she desired. To reinvest her time and energy to create a path out of her career, so when the timing was right, she could leave.

This self-made suffering continued for over five years and she never took ACTION on my advice. This was long before I knew what I shared earlier about having useless conversations. I could have used that time for something else, instead of pouring it into someone that refused to take part in their own rescue.

Without taking ACTION to change her circumstances, she got caught in a negative cycle. Her stress and anxiety became unmanageable, so she started smoking. She started drinking regularly to alleviate the pain of her world and this caused headaches, high blood pressure and migraines.

In order to ease her depression, she ate high calorie, high fat comfort foods and gained weight. Since her weight gain became an issue in the organization, she started smoking more and became rail thin. The toxic cocktail of chemicals that ran through her system caused the texture of her skin to change. The tremendous amount of stress and anxiety that *indecision* caused pretty much fried her decision making faculties, so she just became more and more miserable which resulted in a variety of illnesses.

From her perspective, she was working in a toxic environment. Her coworkers, in three different offices, would likely say she was creating the toxic environment. Every supervisor had it out for her and she felt like she had a bulls-eye on her forehead. In her mind, there was a dark cloud around her and everyone was out to get her.

But why did she stay if she was going nuts? What was the real reason for going through all of that and refusing to change?

S-E-C-U-R-I-T-Y. A government salary is like the sweet tea I love. Refreshing, crisp, and delicious. It's secure, consistent, and she's near the six-figure mark. She's accumulated a lifestyle that's hard to break away from. Golden Handcuffs, choosing the security of a paycheck over everything else in life. Creating a lifestyle around a salary, but then choosing to keep the lifestyle, even if the job that pays the salary is choking her out.

Can you relate to this story? Do you feel stuck in your job and then call it Golden Handcuffs?

**Most People Worldwide Dislike Their Jobs**
I went into great detail to highlight her story because she's not alone in this scenario. The majority of people around the world have discontent for their jobs. Gallup's " 2013 State of the Global Workplace," revealed 87 percent of workers worldwide "are emotionally disconnected from their workplaces and are less likely to be productive." Eighty-seven percent!!!

Only 13 percent of workers felt engaged by their jobs and were passionate about their work. Sixty-three percent are not engaged and are checked out and 24 percent pretty much hate their jobs. These people act out and undermine their co-workers.

If 87 percent of people are emotionally disconnected from their workplaces, they are susceptible to stress, anxiety and depression, and their related illnesses kill millions of people each year. Stress can cause or exacerbate high blood pressure, diabetes, obesity, asthma, migraines, depression, gastrointestinal problems, accelerated aging and premature death. The young lady mentioned above is well on her way to digging an early grave.

There are tons of books, articles, and blogs about what companies should do to engage their workers in order to motivate them to be more productive. My preference is to start with the man/woman in the mirror. So many people are waiting for someone else to motivate them, manage them better, or quit (we are relieved when bad bosses leave).

They want others to manage their stress for them, or their workload. To somehow magically bestow work-life balance on them. Thousands of people are dying every day from preventable stress related conditions, because they are waiting for someone else to change.

Paraphrasing Dr. Wayne Dyer, "If other people have to change before you can be happy, you would have to send the whole world to the psychiatrist."

When you are unhappy, stressed and depressed, you are the only one that can save yourself. It starts with a DECISION. Without deciding, your family can't save you. Neither can your spouse, children, co-workers, friends, and/or a therapist. **You are going to have to save yourself!**

People have resulted to drugs, alcohol and other narcotics to alleviate their pain of not making a DECISION. Alleviating these conditions with chemicals will numb you from the pain, but it will not change your condition. You have to get to the root cause of what's causing these conditions and then resolve it at the root to free yourself. Otherwise, you will spend the best part of your life numbing conditions that can be changed with a DECISION and ACTION!

## Take Responsibility For Your Results

It's easy to look at outside circumstances and blame them for causing your problems, grief, anxiety or depression. Yet, the hardest thing to do is to look in the mirror and take 100% responsibility for what's good and bad in your life.

> *"Spend 5 minutes complaining and you've wasted 5."*
> *– Jim Rohn*

Nearly four years ago, I was miserable, sick, felt unlovable and was disconnected from my family and friends. It was easy to blame my bosses, nasty ex-coworkers, dysfunctional family members and bad relationships for my problems. But, were they really the problem?

The only constant in the story that I played over and over again in my head was me. I was the one who continued to stay with an organization after being treated adversely for years. I made the decision to stay and excelled professionally, but it came with great sacrifice. So, what's the real story?

1. The money was awesome.
2. I loved my job and only had bad bosses every few years.
3. I was a workaholic and drove my health into the ground, because I didn't take care of myself and manage my stress.

4. My biggest challenge was expecting for people to respect me and when they didn't, I would get irate or self-combust.
5. I lost the ability to value myself and my contributions when I changed my preferences and personality in order to get good performance evaluations.
6. Since I worked in a male dominated environment, I was used to being aggressive and in charge. I didn't know how to turn it on and off and it became a part of who I was.
7. The men I dated didn't like a woman who carried the energy of a man, so I was single for a good part of my career.

That is only a small percentage of the true story, because all of those story lines had a background and long line of reasons. My intent is to convey to you that stories, issues and circumstances are not one dimensional. They have layers, upon layers of stuff that we have gotten spun around in. Once you choose to take responsibility for your life, you'll understand that there are extenuating circumstances to the story that you are playing in your head and what's keeping you from moving forward.

You are the only one that can save yourself! But you can only save yourself if you choose to take responsibility for every result that you have right now. If you don't like where you are, you are the only one that can change it. If you want to be happier than you are right now, you are the only one that can do it. If you want to become greater than you are right now, you are the only one that can do it.

So many times, we put our happiness in the hands of others and are greatly disappointed when they don't measure up. We can't control others, we can only control ourselves.

Once you get clear on your goals, the life you want to live and where you want to be, taking responsibility for your results will become easier. Once you know where you're going, you'll know which friends won't get you there. Once you understand how you want to feel, you'll understand that holding on to guilt and unforgiveness won't get you that feeling and you'll have to make a choice. Once you start feeding your dreams and your destiny, you'll eventually understand that looking back is counterintuitive and you'll have a choice to make. What choice will you make?

**Today Is A Blank Slate**

One image that I found useful in recreating my life and not looking back was to imagine that every day was a blank canvas. With a blank sheet of paper, crayons and markers, I had the ability to create what I wanted that day. Yesterday is gone and can't be changed. Today, I have the ability to create my tomorrow. What will I do today that will make me happier tomorrow?

I wrote TODAY on a blank sheet of paper and hung it on the wall near my bedroom door, because that's generally the wall I look at when I wake up. I needed to be reminded right as I opened my eyes, that today was blank slate.

At night, usually disappointed in something that didn't get done, or someone who got on my nerves, I would spend time lamenting about it, when I should've been sleeping. This exercise was useful because I knew the next day, I had another blank slate and an opportunity to do it again.

I recommend you do the same. It's a simple, yet very powerful exercise.

## Tame The Negative Voice

A lot of emotions can be triggered by self-talk and the voice in your head. You know the one I'm talking about...the tyrant that talks to you the moment you decide to step outside of your comfort zone and do something new. The voice that shows up and tells you that you don't know what you are doing, you'll fail or you're a loser. Sometimes, its beats you down, and talks you out of doing something before you even begin. Yes, THAT voice.

Self-talk (self-criticism) is one of the most destructive behaviors/habits that we have. There is an on-going story in most of our heads that reflect the reality of our greatest fears. It also comes from the opinions and criticism of others we've collected over the years.

Imagine your mind as a tape recorder. You are the tape recorder and not the tape. If you choose, you can eject the current tape and replace it with another one that tells the story of the life you want.

If you choose to take control of your mind, the voice in your head can be trained. It will take some time to retrain the voice, but if you are still living next year, the time will pass anyway. Why not use it to better your life? If you recognize there is a voice talking to you, what's the harm in talking back to it? *Haa haa!*

Some people may reject that notion immediately, but it is better to talk back to the voice in your head and fight for the life you want, than to let it control you and live in misery.

Let's test it. Please repeat the following statements that pertain to you aloud and internalize them if they are things you really want. Pause….and observe what the voice says to you.

1. I want a better job.
2. I want to be healthier.
3. I want to make more money.
4. I want to be happier.
5. I want better relationships with my family and friends.

Was the voice supportive? Did it say something you didn't agree with? Would you have liked a better response? Again, it is possible to reprogram your mind, but you will have to become more aware of what you are saying to yourself, so you need to become an observer.

In the phenomenal book *Psycho-Cybernetics*, Dr. Matthew Maltz gives 5 Steps for Reprogramming the voice. Observing your inner voice, when it says something negative, do the following (CRAFT):

1. Cancel – say it aloud
2. Replace – with positive data
3. Affirm – the new image you desire
4. Focus – 10 minutes daily
5. Train – yourself for lasting change.

When I first started practicing CRAFT, I would shout "cancel" aloud in the grocery store. Although I may have startled some people, they kept it moving and I became better for it. ☺

## Signs of Impending Burnout

Are you on the road to burning out or digging an early grave? I'm asking you this because of my personal experience. Four years ago I burned out so bad it wasn't even funny. I refused to take anti-anxiety medication, but drank wine daily for six months to numb myself from how much my life sucked. I decided that drinking to mask a **DECISION** I wasn't willing to make was lunacy.

Looking back, had I known then what I knew now, I would have left a lot sooner. This is why I'm so passionate about what I do and say. Staying for the check and salary will kill you far faster than starting over fresh in the unknown.

Several signs of burnout can include: prolonged and regular headaches, panic attacks, exhaustion, feelings of hopelessness, being disorganized, ringing ears and regular colds (which reflects a suppressed immune system).

Alcohol, prescription or illicit drugs will only numb you from what will eventually happen. Physical or mental breakdown or death. Doctors will quickly write you a prescription for anti-anxiety medication and a therapist will talk to you until your head pops off, but there is a "rip off the Band-Aid" way to free yourself and people rarely give that advice, if ever.

***The best way to turn around burnout is to leave the situation that's causing it!*** Often, we hold on to the very thing that's killing us, because leaving (job, relationship, marriage, situation) will subject us to criticism.

Burnout comes when a DECISION is being avoided. Instead of making the hard decision, our bodies consistently emit a toxic cocktail of chemicals and erupt in disease and discomfort. Deteriorating health is our bodies screaming take ACTION, but taking action to do the impossible and the unthinkable takes courage.

There are people who have died at their desk, because they chose to hold on to the image of who they thought they were and what they meant to an organization. They failed to make the DECISION to put themselves and their families first and because of that, they paid a high price. Don't let this be you.

# Small Tweaks – Big Results
# Take Ownership

Have you set any goals for yourself lately? Not easy goals, but goals worth failing for. Would you like to achieve more personal and professional goals, have better relationships, and get control of your stress, anxiety or depression?

To do this, it's important to focus on what you want and not on what you don't want. Instead of focusing on having less anxiety, focus on having more peace. Instead of focusing on your past bad relationships, focus on the characteristics of your dream mate.

## Action Steps

**1. Be Willing To Grow** – Dr. Maltz said, "Anything that has been learned can be re-evaluated and challenged. Anything that has been challenged can be 'relearned' with new data to replace the old." Answer the following questions for yourself:

a)  What are some things you would like to change?

b)  What's the story in your head that keeps you from living the life you desire?

c)  What are the reasons you can't live the life you desire?

d)  Even if you had an actual event, incident or health condition that stopped you from achieving something, does telling the story over and over again (to yourself or others) serve you?

e)  When you retell the story, how does it make you feel?

f)  How many times have you told that story?

g)  Are you tired of hearing your own story or will it be your story until you pass on into the next life?

Free yourself from that story and create a new life, with richer experiences, less baggage, more sunlight, better tasting food and fresher air. It's MAGICAL!

**2. Set Clear Goals** – When you set a clear vision for what you want, you have something to work towards, and a reason to get out of bed in the morning. Write your vision on notecards and hang them in your bathroom mirror. Have another set at your desk. That way, your goals are always in front of you.

Take 30 mins to an hour and think about what you want your life to look like in the next:

a) Two months
b) Six months
c) Twelve months
d) Two years
e) Five years

| Action | Date | Notes |
|---|---|---|
| Read | | |
| Understand | | |
| Apply | | |
| See Change | | |
| Pedal to the Medal | | |

# Chapter 4

# *God Is Real*

*"There is a plus-entity and minus-entity in every human body that is born into the world. Whichever one of these is favored by the flesh becomes dominant; then is the other inclined to abandon its habitation, temporarily or for all time."*
*– Fredrick Van Rensselaer Dey*

I'm not a religious person and actually ran away from organized religion for an extended time. Going to small churches that taught about God from the Old Testament didn't make me feel good. The vibrations were low and I usually felt small and minimized after leaving. Always hearing that God was a jealous God and that I would be punished with hell, fire and brimstone if I didn't abide by what seemed like impossible standards was scary. Not only that, to see so called "sanctified people" talk about people on an epic level and do negative things to others, but go to church faithfully every Sunday, just turned me off all together. I became an atheist.

Over a 20-year period, I didn't acknowledge that God existed, but would call upon him when I got into real deep trouble. Yes, a hypocrite I know, but please stick with me. I prayed for healing when I was crippled with arthritis and was fully healed, without medication. I prayed for several other things and after a series of showing up when I needed Him and then denying Him after I got it, one day I thought, "Maybe there is something to God, but how do I get back?"

For a long time, I thought that highly spiritual people were weird, but they had peace and I had chaos, so who was the real weirdo? Then, I became tired. Life was wearing me out and had put a whooping on me. I felt a positive energy that was pulling me and urging me to get closer. But closer to what? What is it? Who is God? What is He and what can He do for me?

Being introduced to spiritual teachers by Oprah, her guests included Dr. Wayne Dyer, Eckhart Tolle, Lois Hay, Dr. Maya Angelou, Abraham Hicks and Gary Zukav. They talked about an energy, a Being, the source, the universe....God. The Being they talked about wasn't the hell and brimstone person that would cast down the heavens, and burn me up if I ever sinned. They spoke of love, openness and acceptance.

After hearing about this loving Being over six years ago, I secretly declared that I wanted to be closer to God and set out on a path to make something happen. I was unsure of how to get closer to something I didn't understand. I started on a journey of relationship and not religion. There is a huge difference between religion and relationship.

**Relationship Is Personal**

I'm still an amateur on the Bible and will not claim to be a spiritual teacher, but I want to give an account of my personal experience. Really just an introduction, and the rest will be expanded in future books. It's not my intent to offend, discredit, criticize or demean anyone, their religion or beliefs. We are all individual beings and will have personal experiences on who we choose to worship and how we choose to worship them.

The day that I decided to resign from my career, I lay in the bed crying from the pain of arthritis that exploded in my ankle due to the extreme stress in my job. I was at a crossroads.

A voice from within said, "Put your gloves down Christy. It's time to stop fighting."

I answered the voice aloud and said, "Okay, I surrender."

That was the beginning of when I *consciously acknowledged* there was another presence with me. I *consciously acknowledged* and answered the inner voice that had been speaking to me for years. I had sensed there was someone with me, guiding me, but I didn't listen to them. The One that was meant to guide and protect me from harm.

Have you heard an inner voice? Not the negative voice or the one that rattles your nerves, but the one that gives you peace. A whisper....the still small voice.

As I continued to grow on my spiritual journey, I remembered the voice actually talked to me many times before that day. Years earlier, I was at home sleep one night and the voice said, "Don't answer that."

I woke up and said, "Answer what?" Then the phone rang and I answered it. It was trying save me from 18 months of heartache from a bad relationship.

A few months before resigning, I was under tremendous pressure and drove my sports car dangerously fast, bobbing and weaving down the interstate. The voice said, "Christy, slow down. You are driving dangerously and you're going to get yourself or someone else killed."

I answered the voice and said, "Yeah, yeah, yeah.... I know." Nearly a week later, I was pulled over three times in seven days. Three times in seven days!!! Obviously, someone or something was trying to get my attention and after that, I was finally ready to listen. It made me slow down, take a pause and realize that I was indeed going too fast on multiple occasions, and that the stress gave me the need for speed. I realized then I needed to start listening and heeding what it was guiding me to do.

Have you ever heard an inner voice talk to you? Can you note when you followed it and saw it may have saved you from an accident or dangerous scenario? Can you note when you didn't follow it and suffered?

## Too Distracted To Listen

Most of us are too distracted to hear the still small voice within. If we have 10 conversations going on in our head at the same time, it's difficult to distinguish if there is someone trying to reach us. Also, negative experiences from our past can keep a perpetual negative conversation going in our head.

With the rise in technology, we have access to the inner thoughts and feelings of millions of people around the world, and an endless stream of atrocities being broadcasted on the news 24 hours a day. We are exposed to more in one day than people in the early 1900's were exposed to in a lifetime. Some people don't consider that a bad thing, but the rise in depression, suicides and drug overdoses tell a different story.

There was a time when the only people we were connected to were those who we could remember their phone numbers. Also, there wasn't an *immediate* expectation that we would talk to them or return their call, because we didn't know they called if we weren't home. I'm really going to show my age here. But, this was before caller ID and answering machines. If you're over 35, do you remember this time?

We had two to five close friends. Then, answering machines and caller ID came along, but we still had the opportunity to get back with them in a few days, because they didn't know when we checked the message. There wasn't an expectation to have an *immediate* connection and an *immediate* response to a non-emergency. Non-emergencies didn't constitute and *immediate* phone call or response.

Today, with technology and the "read time stamp," people will get mad if you don't *immediately* respond to their non-emergency. Non-emergencies are a priority and is distracting millions of people from their personal desires. Now we are connected to and responding to hundreds of people's non-emergencies.

Within five minutes of waking up in the morning and before going to bed at night, we are tending to the non-emergencies of people we don't know. Thousands of people are killed in car accidents each year for having non-emergency conversations texting while driving.

How can you figure out who you are and where you are going if you are always connected to others? How can you be connected with yourself, if you are connected to hundreds of people? How can you be connected with your inner being, your inner sense of self, your inner me, the God within, if you are busy responding to non-emergencies of hundreds of people that you know and thousands that you don't know on social media?

## Getting Still For Purpose and Destiny

When we get to a certain point in life, we are ready to figure out who we are and why we're here. Millennials seem to have this desire naturally, but Gen X's are coming into this stage. We were all put here to accomplish something great and that task is as individual as our fingerprint. This has nothing to do with money, and is meant to serve and make a great impact in the lives of others. Some contributions will be in a family, others in a community, some nationally and a few internationally.

This is all determined by what you're willing to hear, the actions you're willing to take and the sacrifices you're willing to make to BECOME who you were meant to be. A lot of people won't *hear* or *feel* the call, because they're too busy. A lot of people won't *answer* the call, because they don't recognize who's calling. Lastly, a lot of people won't *heed* the call, because they're too afraid.

I talked to a college classmate about destiny and he asked me how to find his Purpose and how he would know that it was actually his Purpose. I asked him a few questions and he told me his dream was to create a youth band in his local community. I then asked him to tell me his vision, what he would do and a few other questions to assess his passion. He got really excited as he described it to me in great detail, and with a vivid imagination.

What he wanted to do was crystal clear. He told me how he would do it, what they would do and how it would impact the kids and the community. He went on and on for nearly 10 minutes. I then asked if his heart was beating fast, he said, "Yes."

"That's your Purpose," I said.

"But how will I do it?"

"If you could do it on your own, then it wasn't a vision from God. You will need Him to accomplish it. The HOW is none of your business. But, you have to work to do your part and believe that He will show up to do his part."

He had seen the vision of what he was meant to accomplish and who he was meant to serve and impact during his time here, but got stuck on HOW. He also got stuck on HOW he would transition from his current job and HOW he would afford it.

He was well-versed in reading the Bible, but not well versed in what Napoleon Hill called "Applied Faith." It's actually applying and doing what has been read and cited verbally for years.

"Walk by faith and not by sight."

"All things are possible for those who believe."

"No weapon formed against me shall prosper."

These are all popular sayings of believers, but they are imperative to BELIEVE and APPLY when working towards your Purpose. Walking in Purpose takes supernatural faith and a host of other qualities that can be developed over time. It takes time to BECOME who you were meant to be in an effort to do the work you were called to do. A pot roast cooked in the microwave in 15 minutes would not be as delicious and moist as one cooked in a slow cooker for 8 – 12 hours.

It's never too late to BECOME who you were meant to be.

Samuel L. Jackson didn't get big roles in acting until he was in his 40's.

Vera Wang started designing wedding dresses in her 40's.

Mary Kay Ash started Mary Kay at 45.

Ray Kroc started McDonalds at 52.

## The Call May Be Misinterpreted

*Shackled To Success*, shared the progression that led to me BECOMING who I am today and having the clarity to share this information with you. Of course it flows now, because I'm sharing it in hindsight, but while being called and actually CHOOSING to answer the call, it was traumatic.

I'm not saying this to scare you or intimidate you from answering the call, but sometimes people see the outrageously negative events and injustices in their lives as punishment, not realizing it is the breaking needed to get on another path. The path, the right path...His path.

If you have been dreaming about starting a business, changing jobs or being a better parent, how would you feel about being blindsided with getting laid off from your successful career? Would it rock your world or would you see it as the avenue to leave your job and do something different? You got what you wanted, it just didn't happen the way you imagined.

As stated earlier, years ago I started envisioning my future and what I wanted my life to look like after retirement. I planned to retire, and then start the vision of my heart. It was going to be perfect. I would have a guaranteed pension, security, money saved, well laid out plans, and all the connections and network that I needed to live the vision. I loved my job, but wanted a different personal life.

I became crystal clear on my future, which is actually the life that I live today, but this life came from my reality being interrupted, and my highly successful career being pretty much burned to the ground. Aaaaallll the way to the ground!! Lol!

The trajectory of my life had been interrupted. The script that I had planned and laid out had been erased by a series of negative (and at times outrageous) events. I was thrust into my Purpose.

I was given the opportunity to actually do what I had been envisioning and not wait for the circumstances to be perfect. *The circumstances will NEVER be perfect!* You have to go ALL IN to fulfill the vision of your heart!

You have everything you need right now to BECOME who you were meant to be. But, it's a choice on whether or not you will answer the voice and do the work. It takes courage to live the life you imagine and it's absolutely worth it. Are you ready?

**Finding The Way Back**

There are a gazillion people ready and willing to teach you the word of God. There are small churches, mega churches, virtual churches, spiritual teachers, podcasts, websites, etc. How you learn should be based on personal preference and personal desires. Also, who you are and what you want to do with your life.

Some people love small churches, and others prefer mega churches. I'm personally not a fan of small churches. I didn't like to stand up and announce my name and where I was from to an established congregation of people that I thought were secretly judging me. I didn't like to see the same people fall out on the floor every Sunday, because I was secretly judging them. I didn't like to be in a church where people spoke in tongues, because I found it highly distracting.

Although I was highly successful in my career, I didn't know any scriptures and felt like dummy for not knowing the fundamental rituals of church.

As a leader, I always had to be conscious of how I was perceived by others. I lost my sense of self during my career and didn't want people talking to me or asking me questions in church, even though they were nice.

I was self-conscious and wanted to experience God, but didn't want people to see me doing it, since I didn't do it like them. I wasn't loud and didn't talk. I didn't fall out or speak in tongues. I didn't understand why people raised their hands. I didn't want to raise my hands. I didn't have a Bible, because I didn't know how to find the verses.

One day, I watched Pastor Joel Osteen on television in 2009. I was hooked, because he didn't quote a bunch of scriptures. He taught how to live a better, more expansive and greater life. I watched his shows periodically and when I moved to Texas a few years later, I drove 1.5 hours to his church a few Sundays a month.

I loved the idea that the church was huge and no one knew me personally. The attendees were there for their experience and since it was so many people in the room, my paranoia of not knowing what I was doing melted away.

The ushers and greeters were nice and they didn't know my "perceived importance from my job," so I could relax and be human again. I wasn't a leader in church. I was a vulnerable human looking for God.

After leaving Texas, I streamed his services live from their website. Over the past three years, I've expanded and also watch Bishop TD Jakes and Pastors John Gray, Joyce Meyer and Steven Furtick. They each have a unique way of teaching and I thoroughly enjoy them.

I can honestly say that watching a multitude of videos from these spiritual teachers has transformed my life and also the connection with God. They are loved by millions all over the world, but interestingly enough, they are also highly criticized by others.

Walking in God's Purpose has not spared them from the burden that comes with higher positions of authority and blessings, but I'm glad they persevered through their process and broke the mold in order to Become who they were meant to be in order to serve who they were meant to serve.

You don't have to go to church to get closer or come into relationship. You also don't have to walk around quoting scriptures, wear a cross and carry a Bible to get into relationship. It's a personal choice and a personal journey, but learning from other spiritual teachers is the key.

If you don't have a church home, feel out of place and aren't sure about who God is and how He wants to show up in your life, take a look at some of the videos and teachings of the leaders I provided above or choose your own. Regardless, make an effort to learn more.

**Relationship Takes Time**

Getting into a relationship with God is similar with being in a personal relationship with the person of your affection. There is a wooing as you are being called. As you spend more and more time with Him, you will develop a closeness and a bond. Do the work and get to know Him and in doing so, you will get to know more about yourself. You will discover commonalities and areas that will need to be worked on in order for the relationship to work and be harmonious. Will you pursue Him in the same manner you pursued your spouse or the same way you plan to pursue the person of your dreams when you meet them?

*"I am the plus-entity of yourself; you are the minus-entity. I own all things; you possess naught. That body which we both inhabited is mine, but it is unclean and I will not dwell within it. Clean it, and I will take possession."*
*– Fredrick Van Rensselaer Dey*

Be patient with yourself and allow your life to unfold in divine order. Spiritual development can't be microwaved and I'm not sure if you want it fast. It takes time to BECOME and remember you are elevated with tests and trials. So if you want it fast, expect to be in extreme trials at all times. No one wants that.

As you continue to grow and develop, expect tests. That means, expect to have hard times. If you understand you can't get to the next level without passing the tests, then challenges and unbelievable situations will be seen from a different perspective.

Challenges are meant to be moved and grown through. They aren't meant to hinder you from your destiny. What is God trying to teach you and get you to understand about yourself? What situation or circumstance seems to be a recurring theme in your life? Do you feel like you are going around and around on an issue and you can't seem to get past it? What are you doing differently that will get you out of that cycle?

Only by changing your reaction can you change the circumstance. If you react the same way each time, you won't be able to progress.

For a good part of my life, I had anger issues. I didn't walk around angry all the time, but had a short fused temper for certain things. I didn't like to feel like I had been disrespected, downplayed and I didn't like for people to try to hustle me. Otherwise, I'm pretty rational, but in those cases and several others, I can be considered irrational.

A few years ago while moving on the journey to destiny, I learned that in order to BECOME who I was meant to be in this world, there was no room for my short fused temper. Especially in a world of cynics and critics who are looking for a reason to attack others, my temper would easily get me in trouble.

Not only would my image be smeared, but my health would also be greatly affected until I finally changed my default. I was nice to a certain point, but after that point, I couldn't be held responsible for what happened.

A few years ago, I was working with this person on a project and had paid them several thousand dollars to complete it. When they missed the deadline for the third time, I became irate. I maintained myself well the first two times, and was pretty proud. All of that went out of the window and my calm demeanor quickly deteriorated and the anger escalated into numerous expletives.

The fourth time the deadline was missed, I went BANANAS! The fifth time, I thought I was going to have a heart attack. If I would have had this person's address, I would have rode by their house and thrown bricks through their windows. I was SO MAD!!!! All of my money was wrapped up in this project and they wouldn't complete it, delaying everything I wanted in my life.

God was using this person like sandpaper on me. The hard, gritty kind. During this tumultuous time, I watched a particular episode of TD Jakes three times and on the third time, I heard something that I had not heard before. I had to watch it again to fully grasp the concept and what was said.

He talked about why Moses didn't get into the Promise Land. It was because of his temper. Realizing that all things work together and I seemed to be getting nowhere with my reaction, I wondered if this particular episode kept coming up in my que for a reason. Hmmmm.....was God trying to tell me something? Was I available and open enough to hear it? Was I conscious enough to set aside my ego and apply it?

It was a tough choice to make, but realizing that I was going in circles, I knew I had to do something different. In order to avoid this person, I created a bridge between us and brought in one of my business partners to communicate on my behalf. I was no longer capable of having a sensible conversation, and needed someone that could communicate effectively, so we could move the project forward. That fell through and I finally had to have a conversation with this person and let them know we had to terminate the project. I was not happy at all, but I wasn't angry either.

That experience was one of the most excruciating experiences I remember when it came to holding on to what I wanted and not surrendering it for a higher Purpose. I liked having a crazy woman buried within me one to two levels down. Lol! *Seriously...please don't act like this person doesn't exist in you.*

As a kid, I was known as the person that when you pushed me hard enough, I would turn into the Hulk and become invincible. I carried this person with me for a looooong, time, but in order for me to get to where I was going and who I was Becoming, that inner being had to be annihilated.

I felt that it was dramatic and traumatic, but looking back, my unwillingness to let it go, while still wanting to ascend and build a stronger relationship with God is what made it so hard. I've learned to be more intuned and keyed in on attributes that may be undesired, and surrender them more willingly and a lot easier. Otherwise, I would continue to go around and around to get to the next level. I like the quicker and less painful way.

Annihilating my anger issues has served me well and has completely changed the relationships I have with people, including my family. Thinking of the story told in Chapter 1 of me not responding to negative people, that ending would have been different and I wouldn't be writing this book, had I not surrendered my temper to get to a higher level.

What issue continually plagues you? What has you going in circles? Can you surrender your will for a higher purpose and better plan?

**Gratitude Gets Results Faster**

Are you grateful for what you have today? When is the last time you've expressed gratitude for what you currently have? Some people pray for a bigger house, but aren't grateful for the three-bedroom house they currently have.

1. Do you remember living in an apartment with loud neighbors and a dog that barked constantly?
2. Do you have enough today to meet your current needs?
3. Are you healthy?
4. Do you sleep in a bed at night?
5. Do you have furniture?
6. Do you have the capacity to get out of bed unassisted?
7. Can you see?
8. Can you hear?
9. Can you walk?
10. Can you talk?
11. Are you able to digest your food properly?
12. Are you able to drive to work and walk up the stairs to get to your office?
13. Are you able to walk into a store, get the groceries you need and pay for them?

Yes, these seem like basic things to people, but it's not a reality for everyone. According to the Census Bureau, only 20 percent of households make over $100,000 a year. It seems like the more money we make, the less grateful we are for the small things.

I wasn't grateful for walking until I was crippled with arthritis and walking became very painful. I wasn't grateful for waking up in the morning, because I got a headache thinking about the day ahead. I wasn't grateful for being able to talk until I started losing my voice every December for 10 days, because of mold exposure in my previous career.

We miss today's miracle while praying for tomorrow's desire. If we are so busy looking at what we want (more money, bigger house, nicer car, a spouse, better clothes), we are missing what we already have.

As shared earlier, money doesn't equal happiness, but if you can take inventory of what you already have, then it may quell your longing for more. It may allow you to see that you already have what you desire, and you will feel more accomplished than you do now. Seeing what you have now will also allow you to view how far you've come in your life.

The media and retailers make us feel like we are missing out on happiness and life without what they are selling. Buy this car and you'll be as happy as the people in the commercial. But this watch and you'll be admired by all the men in your office. Buy this house and you'll be the talk of the town. Spend a gazillion dollars on a wedding and be the envy of all your friends.

But what about the things you already have? What about the things that you were given at birth for free that you exchanged for money and success? What about inner peace, sound physical health, and joy. A close connection and quality time with family and friends?

What are you trying to fix with outer things and material possessions? Are you praying for everything outside of yourself, when what you really need is to fix what's going on within you?

Once you're able to give gratitude for what you have, you'll get clarity on the small things that really make you happy. Do you really need an expensive watch to validate your worth or can you actually see you have a problem valuing your self-worth and that's what you really need to focus on?

**"Perfection is a disease of a nation… Trying to fix something, but you can't fix what you can't see. It's the soul that needs the surgery."**
**- Beyonce**

I started keeping a gratitude journal in 2009. Before going to bed each night, the goal was to write down five things I was grateful for. Initially, I was very shallow and hadn't really taken inventory of what I already had. I wrote down stuff like, ice cream, no rain, new shoes, a good hair day, spending time with my friends, a lemon drop martini, sweet tea, and delicious sweet potato fries. *Hey, you have to start somewhere.*

Over time, I started to see more stuff to be grateful for like health, the ability to walk, spending time with my family, having a steady income, getting another certification at work. Now, I'm grateful for the smallest things like, the wind blowing through my hair, surviving this unfoldment, having passion for life, perfect health, inner peace, God's grace, self-love, freedom from fear and good dark chocolate.

As with everything, this takes action and practice in order to see how the effects will change your life. Will you give it a try? Are you willing to be grateful for your desires that have already been answered, rather than be frustrated, because what you want next isn't coming fast enough?

# Small Tweaks – Big Results
# God Is Real

Do you want a closer connection with God? As you continue to read this book, I will offer additional insight into how to become less distracted. Clearing your mental clutter will open up your head and heart space.

## Action Steps

**1. Find Your Purpose** - Are you looking for your Purpose or have a yearning to do more, but you're unsure of what it is? Take 15-30 minutes of uninterrupted time to consider and answer the following questions. Really give them some thought and write your answers down.

   a) What would you do if all of your lifestyle expenses were paid?

      1. What would you do for free?

      2. Does that excite you and make your heart race?

      3. Does it serve others?

   b) What do you do for others regularly for free?

      1. What are you known for in your family and community?

      2. What do people call you for?

   c) What have you heard from the inner voice?

      1. What have you seen in a vision or dream?

      2. Did it scare you?

      3. Can you do it alone?

      4. Would it be considered outrageous by others?

**2. Determine If You Want Religion Or Relationship** - What are you willing to do to get it? How much time are you willing to invest in getting to know yourself? The more time you spend looking within, the faster results you'll get. Can you turn off the television and spend less time on social media to get reacquainted with yourself?

**3. Choose Expansion and Growth** - Expand your awareness and consciousness of God, the universe, the Source or however you choose to acknowledge the higher power. Get a video or a book from Oprah, Wayne Dyer, Eckhart Tolle, Lois Hay, Maya Angelou, Gary Zukav, Joel Osteen, John Gray (Pastor), TD Jakes, Joyce Meyer and/or Steven Furtick. I have a longer list, but these leaders are my favorite.

**4. What Do You Need To Work On** - Start to become aware of the issues that you are having a hard time overcoming. What can you do differently? Write down the scenarios and your reactions to them. What is the common thread?

**5. Keep A Gratitude Journal** - It doesn't have to be fancy, but since it's a ritual, you may want to get a nice hardback journal. They sell them at all major retailers, but discount and dollar stores also have small journals at a low price. Write down the date and five things you are grateful for that day. There is no right or wrong way to do this, so don't judge yourself. I was grateful for a lemon drop martini....soooo, there definitely isn't judgment here.

**6. Meditate** - Meditating offers significant benefits as it calms your mind and reduces the number of voices and stories fighting for space in your head. Meditation not only lowers your blood pressure, but can also amp up your immune system while improving your ability to concentrate. There are tons of meditation apps and videos on YouTube. Give chanting or Om's a try to vibrate the negative energy off of you. It takes time to train your mind to slow down, so be patient. Start with five minutes, three times a week. If you can't sit in silence, try guided meditations. As you start to see progress, increase the time and frequency.

| Action | Date | Notes |
|---|---|---|
| Read | | |
| Understand | | |
| Apply | | |
| See Change | | |
| Pedal to the Medal | | |

Check out my e-course *"How To Unlock Your Amazing Destiny – 10 easy steps."* This course was designed to find the common thread with your reaction to others and how you may feel like you are going around and around on issues. It's also designed to get to the root cause of what's stopping you from feeling fulfilled and will assist you with overcoming the story that plays in your head that stops you from living in your full potential.

Remove your unknown and buried obstacles and get on the road to destiny! www.christyrutherford.com/programs..

# Chapter 5

# *Mind Your Business*

*"You never can afford to condemn another because in his shoes you would probably have done just as badly."*
*- Emmet Fox*

My life changed COMPLETELY when I decided to mind my own business. I didn't realize how much I was dipping my nose in other people's business until I stopped. I didn't know how other people affected me until I started to distance myself from them and become a near recluse for a few months. I turned off my phone, disconnected from all social media and only checked my e-mail for five minutes a day.

It's socially acceptable and normal to be in everybody's business. In addition to social media, we stick our noses in family matters and try to assist them with becoming who we think they should be. Talking to friends and listening to their latest woe is me story about their boss, co-worker, spouse or kids. Listening to the random person that tells you about their problems while you wait in line at the grocery store. As a leader, assessing what your personnel are doing in order to adequately mark them on their performance evaluations.

We are systematically set up to be in other people's business. I didn't even get to the multitude of talk shows, reality shows, magazines, websites, blogs and tweets that are ready and willing to allow you into the private lives of others. Also, what they're wearing, what they're saying, who's dating who, who just broke up, and what their kids look like. It's a constant and incessant stream of data all about *other people.*

How can you ever get clear on who you are if you are always looking at and secretly comparing yourself and your life with other people? Are you comparing your marriage with your neighbor's marriage? Are you looking at the snapshot of "happiness" that others are displaying on social media in their non-stop selfies, and wondering why you aren't that happy?

Are you 120 percent sure that your neighbors are really madly in love and have a greater relationship than you and your spouse? Are those people who look happy all the time on social media really happy?

## Glass Houses

I've learned that every minute I spend looking at someone else's life, leaves me with one less minute to look at mine. However, as stated earlier, it's easier to look at and point out what other people are doing wrong in their lives, but it's hard to see what we are doing wrong.

*"More often than not, the things we detest and judge in others are a reflection of things we cannot accept about ourselves."*
*- Iyanla Vanzant*

Well, I heard it, understood it and then applied it. Yikes!! I found out it was true, and from that day my pedal to the medal was to really look at what I didn't like about others and then search for that behavior/trait within myself. Mysteriously and magically, the issue went away with others too.

I dated this guy once and was able to point out EVERY deficiency he had and what he could do better. Yes, I'm willing to admit my ridiculousness in an effort to teach. I remember telling him that I only had two flaws. I didn't like to be told no and he had to pay attention to me. I often wonder why he didn't run away the moment I said that. Lol!

Hidden behind those two flaws that I proudly touted as *only* having, was several hundred minute details and reasons that went into two very large red flags. Okay, maybe not several hundred.....okay...yes, several hundred. As I started to mind my own business and mine my soul for the hidden treasures that would get me closer to my destiny and Purpose, I couldn't believe how much secretly buried junk that I could easily identify in others, but couldn't see in myself.

I'm continually amazed at people who consider themselves "people watchers," and can't see that proudly wearing that label speaks volumes about them and their self-esteem. Of course, this is someone who only thought she had only two flaws, so we'll move on.

To illustrate, take a look at this image. When you acknowledge the faults in others, you fail to see them in yourself. The guy who is overweight is telling the guy who's smoking that he needs to stop, because it's bad for his health. Well, so is being overweight. Is being overweight and smoking bad? Well it depends on who's judging. Doctors, yes. Other overweight people and smokers, maybe....but not so much.

If they are okay with who they are and the habits they have, do they really need you harassing them about it? The key here is to recognize what YOU can be doing better. Even if it's not an unhealthy habit like smoking, are you stressed out? Do you not spend time with your kids? Do you drink wine to numb yourself to how your life sucks?

The same time that it takes to look at the flaws in others, should be invested in seeing what you can clean up in your own life. You'll find that the more work you do on yourself, the less others will bother you.

**Social Media Hate**

Advances in technology have allowed us to connect with more people than ever before. It's also created new trends and allows people with the same mindsets and ideals to connect. Some of these connections have created movements that have been beneficial, however, other connections have proved to be detrimental. One of the most dangerous trends I've noticed is when people use their collective voices to humiliate, ridicule and destroy others.

The Washington Post published an article, "Whatever Happened to the 15 People The Internet Hated Most in 2015?" Citing, "Scarcely a month went by in 2015 without the christening of some new 'most hated' person... The people change, but the rage cycle remains pretty standard: indignant news coverage, petitions, a tidal wave of online shaming … and then — at last, eventually — nothing. The Internet's rages are passionate and deeply felt, but very quickly forgotten. Which is why, as the year wraps up, it seems important to recount them."

SERIOUSLY!!?? Are we now clocking Hated People like movie reviews? Has society shifted into being "entertained" by destroying someone's life and putting it under a microscope for the whole world to witness their pain, shame and guilt? This is done without regard for their families and creates undue pressure, stress, anxiety and depression. Millions of opinionated strangers suddenly become experts on how a person should live their life.

The persecution of people seems like it's at an all-time high. When people step out of line, make unsavory comments or look at someone with a side eye, the group of collective voices they offend gather together and roar like a speed train. The *social media mafia* (I like to call them) uses multiple social media platforms to steam roll and attack the person. This sort of social media mafia backlash has picked up intensity and maliciousness where it seems like someone is getting burned every week.

Once a person and their families' lives have been dismantled and destroyed, the social media mafia moves on to the next person. Is this now the norm and socially accepted behavior? What are we teaching the next generation? Bullying and teenage suicide trends are unsettling. Coincidence? I think not.

Regardless of whether or not the person of the week being persecuted is right or wrong, innocent or guilty, there are unseen (universal) forces that are activated when you engage in the story of the week. Whether you express opinions, engage in the social media backlash or even watch the videos repeatedly, your life is impacted. Knowing this gives you the choice of whether or not you will participate from this point forward.

Some people don't realize when they create misery in the lives of others, even if they don't know them, it creates unintended consequences in their own lives. With the Law of Attraction, whatever you think about expands. When you take part in criticizing others for their wrongdoing, Karma will respond in kind and you create circumstances in your life to be under scrutiny and criticized as well.

Even though it may not reappear as the exact issue, it may be friction or discourse with your co-workers or supervisors. You may create conflict in your home or personal relationships. People wonder why their kids are being bullied, but don't see how they do it to others. It's like being in a mud-slinging contest, you can't sling opinions and judgment, and not get dirty.

The majority of the people that get dismantled by the social media mafia are highly successful people, who have worked themselves up a ladder; typically, from impoverished conditions to wealth. Viewing highly successful people as inhuman or those that should be held to a higher standard than you, creates a separation between you and them. Backed by the media, this separation causes a pseudo hatred/envy for the money and wealth they have accumulated. If you dislike wealthy and successful people, the Law of Attraction will ensure you repel money and success (responding in kind). You can't hate that which you secretly desire.

Choose to guard your thoughts and be mindful of your opinions about how other people should live their lives. You'll find that your life will change and improve in a short period of time.

## Allowing Others To Affect Your Self-Image

Last year, as I peeled a banana, my brother yelled, "You're doing that wrong!" He watched the video, "Life Hack – You've been peeling a banana wrong your whole life." Although I saw the title, I never watched the video because I didn't have any issues with peeling a banana.

I looked at him for a few seconds and said "Really? I don't care." Annoyed and wanting to state the point, he told me to turn it upside down, pinch the bottom and then peel it. Apparently, that's the way monkeys peel their bananas and feeling slightly dumb, he talked about how he couldn't believe we never really knew how to do it.

Irritated, because peeling a banana is not cause for a heated debate, I did it and found that it was actually easier. However, I've been effectively peeling bananas for over 30 years. I didn't think peeling from the stem like I had always done was wrong, just starting at the bottom was easier. Wrong is an absolute and doesn't leave a lot of options, and to think that we've been peeling bananas wrong our whole lives didn't bode well with me. I thought the advice was useful, but haven't applied it in my everyday life.

Later, as I cut an ice cream cake at Easter dinner, my aunt yelled in a panic, "No, no no, you're cutting it wrong!" With a blank stare, I couldn't believe she had been influenced by these messages. She said, "You should cut going all the way across so you can push the cake together once you're done and it will stay fresher longer."

My aunt has been baking and serving cakes for over 40 years, and I was taken aback that she would say that our normal method of cutting a cake was wrong. I said, "I'm sorry auntie, but I don't remember eating a cake over two days old and this cake isn't going to make it past the next few hours…I think we're okay."

Stating that the whole world had been cutting a cake wrong may have been a catchy title, but as a professional cake eater…ahem, I mean, considered a pretty good cake cutter and pastry chef, I don't think there is a right or wrong way to cut a cake. Cutting hundreds of cakes at special events for work or with the family, is sort of an art.

At the end of the day, recipients of the cake never complained that a piece wasn't symmetrical, not perfectly cut, or looked like it had been sawed into. The comments usually ranged from, "I like the middle." "I like a lot of icing," or "Just give me a small piece."

No one really cared about the way it was cut, and cakes rarely made it out of the event, so was it really "cut wrong" according to the hack video?

Maybe there was a *better way* to cut the cake, but only if the *intention* was the same as the person in the video, which is to save a cake for three to five days. Never, ever a thought for me.

Recently, I've noticed rise in the number of messages that have titles where the language is so absolute and negative that it makes people feel unintelligent.

"10 Hacks You Wished You Thought Of"

"10 Hacks Everyone Must to Know"

"25 Hacks Everyone Should Try"

"35 Things You've Been Doing Wrong All Your Life"

REALLY? Originally coined in 2004, the term "life hack" has risen in popularity and is used across a wide spectrum of subjects. The definition of "hack" is to cut with rough or heavy blows. The definition of "life hack" is a strategy or technique adopted in order to manage one's time and daily activities in a more efficient way. To me, life hack can also be defined as - to cut (life) with rough or heavy blows.

I'm not a fan of the trend, because it seems that the articles and blogs which condescend or demean are opened at a higher rate than those that are meant to uplift and empower. From my own experience, blogs titled with a negative connotation are opened 10 to 1, in contrast to those with a positive vibe.

Have we become motivated by negativity or are we simply trying to find a way to soothe our pain? Are these articles playing a part in the unhappiness that a large number of people are experiencing? Have we become so enthralled with other people's opinions about how we should conduct ourselves, that we've lost sight of what we prefer and what makes us happy?

Of course, this is personal preference, but my goal is to make you aware of how you feel when you read some of these articles or watch the videos. Does it make you feel smarter having learned a new way to do something, or stressed and unintelligent for doing it wrong your whole life? These articles are based on the opinions of others, and although some may be useful, allowing people to influence how you feel about the way you've lived your whole life is shaky ground.

Would you rather spend your energy changing your habit of peeling bananas or expend the same energy forming new habits to be kinder to yourself and manage the negative voice in your head? It takes brain power and a conscious effort to create new habits and the choice is yours.

# Small Tweaks – Big Results
# Mind Your Business

Are you ready to get clarity on who you are and what's stopping you from moving forward? That negative voice in your head feeds off of the small insecurities you carry around and the only way to see the small cracks in your character is to stop looking at other people and put all of your attention on yourself. This will be one of the most important gifts you give yourself.

## Action Steps

**1. Observe Your Inner Voice** - Take note of your inner voice and also your comments to others. Are you judging your family members and others, and do you tell them what they need to do to improve their lives? Are you a people watcher judging someone for having on spandex, crusty feet or dirty shoes?

Do you look at an overweight person and link their weight to the food that's in their shopping cart or their meal at a restaurant? Awareness is the first step to change and once you observe how much you are giving other people, you will see that you have more time in a day than previously thought.

Use that same energy and zero in on some of the deficiencies within yourself that need to be addressed. We're highlighting a number of them in this book, so they will be easier to see.

**2. Social Media Mafia** - When the next scandal of the week is announced, ask yourself the following questions before engaging in it:

    a) Do I know the full story?

    b) Does this affect me personally?

    c) Why do I care?

    d) Have I done something equal to them or worse?

    e) How would I feel if it was me?

        1. What if it was my mom, dad or sibling, how would I feel?

**3. Letting Others Affect You** - Do you let strangers or people give you useless and unsolicited advice? Do you allow them to make you feel differently about yourself?

The next time you come across someone who wants to give you advice, or watch a life hack video, ask yourself the following:

    a) Will I gain useful knowledge from this?

    b) Do I really care?

    c) After reading/watching the hack, do I feel informed or less intelligent?

    d) How did learning this new trait make me feel?

    e) Will I allow others to dictate how I feel about myself?

| Action | Date | Notes |
|---|---|---|
| Read | | |
| Understand | | |
| Apply | | |
| See Change | | |
| Pedal to the Medal | | |

# Chapter 6

# *Evaluate Your Circle*

*"Some of your friends are hitmen sent from hell to take you back. They make you feel bad for wanting to be better. They don't like you because you wanted out of what they were into and they are determined to convince you that there is no other world, but the world they created."*
*- TD Jakes*

It's been said that we are the average of our five closest friends. People who are hourly wage workers hang out together. People who make over $100,000 a year, usually associate with other six-figure earners and wealthy people surround themselves with other wealthy people. People who eat healthy usually hang out together and smokers hang out with other smokers. When you choose to take responsibility for your life and your circumstances, you will need to separate yourself from your closest friends.

This may be unsettling, but if you are looking to leave a secure and steady six-figure career in order to pursue your dreams, you'll be surprised at the resistance you'll get. If you are overweight and REALLY decide to lose weight, can you really enjoy a healthy meal, when your friends are eating their delicious and aromatic high fat, high calorie entrées?

Misery loves company and we tend to surround ourselves with people who share our same dysfunction. This does not make us or them bad people, but some people have accepted their dysfunction as normal and won't do anything about it, because they've numbed themselves to the pain of it.

Having a six-figure career is not dysfunctional by default, but if it's stifling your growth and you spend considerable time sharing woe is me stories with your friends over alcoholic beverages and football games regularly, then it's time to re-evaluate that narrative.

Not only will your current group of friends not do anything for themselves, they will attempt to stop you from changing. When you take action to change, there will be resistance, continued questions and criticism on why you want to break away from the norm of the invisible dysfunction. This DECISION will rest solely with you. Be strong enough and have the courage to take part in your own rescue!

When I decided to leave my successful career, there was considerable backlash and negative comments made by people who I considered to be my friends. They called me stupid, a quitter, and weak. They said "She'll be back."

"Who walks away with only 3.5 years to retire?"

"She only had a year left at that office, she's weak to let someone run her out of her job."

"She was a powerful leader, now she's selling coffee. That's dumb."

On and on. They assumed that I didn't hear what they said, but somehow, their stinging words and criticism continued to make it to my ears.

I can honestly say that leaving everyone I knew for an unknown future was terrifying, but when the people that I cared about turn on me, it was shocking, painful and excruciating.

Looking at who I AM today compared to who I was four years ago, there had to be a breaking. There had to be a separation and isolation from others, because who I AM today is no longer in alignment with who I used to be, and because of that, I no longer have a lot in common with the people I once considered my friends.

They are all highly successful and highly educated, but what I need in friendships today is different than what they're able to give, and that's okay. I had to forsake my past friends to open the channel for friends that would get me to my destiny.

## Clean Your Closet

Are the people you spending your time with getting you closer to what you desire, or are they just hanging around for the sake of hanging around? This is why it's so important to set goals and get clear on the life you desire. Once you get clear on who you are, why you're here and where you're going, you'll know who won't get you there.

It's almost like cleaning your messy closet to prepare for a new and updated wardrobe. Would you take $200,000 and a personal stylist to get a new wardrobe? Would you be willing to reevaluate your existing wardrobe to make room for the new clothes? Ahhhh.....$200,000 for all new clothes, shoes and accessories. How does that make you feel right now? Wouldn't you feel like a brand new person if you were able to get all new clothes? Wouldn't you walk a little taller and strut your stuff?

Just the thought of smelling the new clothes should make you feel refreshed and renewed. But you can't get the money until you make room in your closet. That dress you got from Target isn't as appealing as the one you could get from Armani. Those shoes you got on sale, may not be as appealing at the thought of getting Jimmy Choo's.

But you can't get the new clothes until you make room for them. Can you do that? Looking in your closet and drawers, you have old clothes and some have holes in them. Some are outdated, stained and others are too big or too small. Yet, for some reason, they are predictable and make you feel comfortable. Your clothes that are too small, you secretly hope that you will be able to wear them again, so you hold on to them.

With $200,000 waiting for you, how hard would it be to go through your stuff and get rid of what's stopping you from getting to the next level? How fast would you throw away things that are no longer serving your needs?

The same goes for new friends. Some friends are old, worn out and you've grown out of them, yet, there they are, lingering and taking up space. They are predictable and comfortable, but they have holes and stains in them. Some you put effort into, others you don't, but some you feel you may need one day.

If you want to be refreshed, renewed and walk a little taller, then it's time to treat people who aren't serving you anymore like you would your wardrobe. You may consider this a harsh or unfair comparison, but this is coming from the perspective of someone who has greatly minimized their circle and has become immensely happier, healthier and wealthier for it. I rummaged through the closet and found the true friendships, but that came when I made a complete shift.

If you are comfortable in your misery and are okay with feeling depleted and used, then this scenario will not serve you. But, if you are ready for a change and want to take ACTION to get it, it's time to drink some caffeine and pay attention.

**Fear of Criticism**

Are you hanging around people who limit the possibilities of who you can be? When you tell them your hopes or dreams, do they laugh at you, tell you all the ways you're going to fail or assist you with working out a plan to achieve it?

Research has shown that it takes 14 positive comments to overcome and negate 1 negative comment. So if you tell your friends your dreams and they laugh, it will take 14 positive comments from others or yourself to neutralize the sting from them laughing. Where do you think the negative voices come from in your head that talk you out of doing what you really want to do and going after your dreams?

Knowing this, do you have 14 people that will speak life into you when 1 person speaks fear into you? If not, how much longer are you going to tolerate hanging around people who don't support you?

*"Thousands of men and women carry inferiority complexes with them all through life because some well-meaning but ignorant person destroyed their confidence through opinions or ridicule."*
*- Napoleon Hill*

Speaking to one of my childhood friends a few years ago, I asked him why he looked so tired. He said that he was working two full-time jobs, so he was exhausted. He was also stressed and falling into depression about not having a lot of time to spend with his family and friends. He was overweight and unhealthy, because he didn't have the time or energy to workout. He didn't have time to cook, so his meals were mostly unhealthy fast food.

I asked him why was he working so much, and he said to be able to afford his mortgage. Since he lived alone, I asked, "If you have to work two jobs in order to afford your house, would you consider selling it and moving into smaller house or an apartment? That way, you could downsize to one job and then have ample time to workout and spend time with your family and friends."

He said, "I don't want to look like a failure and make people think I can't afford my house." ☹

Later, I met a 70-year-old lady that had a part-time job at a booth in the mall. She retired a few years ago, but then bought an expensive car. When the payments became too much for her pension, she had to get a job in order to make the payments. She was stressed and overwhelmed because she never thought she would be working at her age. When I asked, "Why not just downgrade to a cheaper car and not have a job?" She said, "I don't want my children to know I bought a car I couldn't afford."

I can go on and on with countless stories of how many people are afraid to change their circumstances for fear of criticism and ridicule by their friends and family. It paralyzes people and makes them do the craziest things and live in misery, simply because they are unwilling to live the life they want to live, regardless of the opinion of others. Most of the time, the fear of criticism is created in the mind and isn't even real.

At the end of the day, we all have our own crap. Sometimes people are criticizing you from their position of strength in certain areas, but also have a vast number of weaknesses in other areas, which you may be strong in. A person may offer criticism on how a healthy person should manage their money, but will turn around and eat a large pizza and half of a cheesecake at one sitting. Hmmmm….

I've learned at the end of the day, the people who truly care about you, want you to be happy. So if you need to drastically change your life in order to do so, they will support you. If my friend sold his house, reduced his jobs and made more time for his friends and family, they would love to see him. Who's going to remember the house 20 years from now?

It takes COURAGE to live the life that you want to live regardless of public opinion and perception. If you make a mistake, it takes COURAGE to change the direction and correct that decision, regardless of how many people will say I told you so. But, some people are willing to live in the mess they created, and would rather suffer the consequences for their decisions (which can be reversed) than suffer the pain of being criticized.

> *"Put your foot upon the neck of the fear of criticism by reaching a decision not to worry about what other people think, do, or say."*
> *– Napoleon Hill*

I read this quote from Napoleon Hill every night for months until it was understood, practiced and became the norm. It takes time to change habits and create new neuro-pathways in the brain, so repetitious information is the key to lasting change.

**Friends Who Limit You**

Be aware of the people who support your goals, all the way up to where they are, because they will turn negative when you surpass what they've accomplished. If you want to be more, do more and have more, you are going to have to make up in your mind that you may be alone for a time in order to accomplish your goals; and that's okay.

There are some people that will try to hold you back so you can continue to serve their needs and their destinies at the expense of yours. In my career, there were people who tied their success to mine, because I was their mentor. However, when it was time for me to go, there was fear and fierce opposition. As a leader, that was tough, but I had a choice to make. Stay behind for them and die, or disappoint them and live. It was a tough decision, but one of the best I've made for me and my family and at the end of the day, that's what counts the most.

Some people believe that if you leave them, they will never see you again and in an effort to keep you in their life, they sabotage you by speaking fear into you. I'm not sure if we are wired wrong, but they don't think they're doing you an injustice when they consciously want to hold you back. They really think they're doing you a favor and saving you from yourself. Millions of people fall for it on a regular basis. But, for you dear reader....Not ANYMORE!

I've seen so many people that are unhappy with themselves and the direction that their life is taking and when I ask why they aren't moving forward, they always point to someone other than themselves and blame them. No one is going to live your life for you. It's the only one you have and you need to ask yourself if you've turned over the steering wheel of your life to someone else and then wonder why you aren't at the destination you desire.

If you are unhappy, while not doing anything about it, can you really be disappointed in others? There are better quality people in the world, but you can't get connected to them, because you are being drug down by the people you won't let go of. Give yourself permission to be happy. Drop the zeroes and run!

I urge you to make the tough DECISIONS and take ACTION to get your life where you want it. Forgive yourself for hurting the people who tied their destiny to the life you are leaving behind and ELEVATE!!

Eagles soar alone and at high altitudes. They don't flock or surround themselves with ducks or chickens. Chickens flock together and are usually on the ground with other chickens. They also eat their own crap. So, as you want to soar and elevate to higher heights, you're going to have to decide if you are going to flock with the multitude of chickens on the ground or soar alone like an eagle.

# Small Tweaks – Big Results
# Evaluate Your Circle

I've heard it said that 90 percent of your friends won't even come to your funeral. Yet, these are the people you are living your life for and allowing to control you. They run your life when you're afraid to be criticized by them and <u>they won't even come to your funeral</u>. I thought the saying was pretty funny, until I saw it play out in real life when one of my good friends died in a car accident.

Of the hundred or so mutual friends we had and those that claimed that he was an incredible friend and colleague, less than 15 showed up for his funeral. I was disappointed, but relieved at the same time, because I had stopped living for others already and was grateful that I didn't have false friendships.

## <u>Action Steps</u>

**1. Evaluate Your Circle -** Are you around people who project their limitations and fears on you when you tell them your lofty goals and dreams? Are you around people who are sucking the oxygen out of you and clip your wings in an effort to "save you from yourself"?

If so, it's time for a season of separation. It's time to discover who you are apart from people who are limiting you. You will be able to grow immensely without them in your life. It's time to clean your closet and surround yourself with people who will breathe life into your goals and encourage you to spread your wings and take flight.

**2. Make A List, Check It Twice:** Get a piece of paper and write down the name of everyone that you consider to be your friend. This also includes family members if you hang around them as peers.

a) When your friends give you unsolicited advice, do you take it blindly or question their motives and intent?

b) How many people do you have in your life that speak fear into you?

c) Who encourages you the most?

d) Who discourages you?

e) Who can you count on at all times?

f) Does the fear of criticism affect your decisions?

g) What are some things you can change today (regardless of criticism) to make your life better?

**3. Meet New People -** Go to Meetup.com and find local events in your area. It's a website and app where people with similar interests get together and hang out. They have a variety of groups such as: bird watchers, cigar smokers, chocolate eaters, bar hoppers, park walkers, board game players, professional networkers, social causes, etc.

New people accept you for who you are and will support you in where you are going. It's time to find like-minded people and fellowship with them.

Lastly, as you start working on your vision, go to personal development conferences and events with people who will assist you with growing your vision.

| Action | Date | Notes |
|---|---|---|
| Read | | |
| Understand | | |
| Apply | | |
| See Change | | |
| Pedal to the Medal | | |

Check out my e-course "Take Inventory – Get flaky people out of your life!" This 30 minute e-course will walk you through how your friends are showing up in your life. It will show you which relationships are one sided, beneficial and who you need to get rid of ASAP!

# Chapter 7

# *All Families Are Dysfunctional*

*"Working on others will not change them. Only by changing yourself will others change."*
*- Neville Goddard*

Nearly five years ago, I was at a yoga studio surrounded by a bunch of compassionate, free-spirited, seaweed chip eating, lemon water drinking, peaceful and calm yogis. I on the other hand, was a highly stressed, giant blueberry muffin and dark chocolate eating workaholic. Lol!

I don't remember the exercise, but we were asked to share our emotions. Numb as a corkboard and with a hardened heart, I had nothing to share. There was one young lady who was bawling her eyes out, because she didn't feel fulfilled in life and couldn't keep a job longer than a year. Her story was pretty tragic UNTIL, she gave the reason for constantly switching jobs. She said, "I can't keep a job because my parents gave me everything I ever wanted." I pretty much checked out of the dialogue earlier, but when she said that, I leaned in closer to ensure my ears were not playing tricks on me.

She said that when she was little, she told her parents she wanted to be a scientist and they bought her a microscope. Then she wanted to be a doctor and they bought her a stethoscope. Then she wanted to be an artist and they bought her an easel and paint. Sobbing loudly at this point, while being surrounded by the other loving yogis, who were also crying and consoling her as she laid out her dreadful childhood, she continued.

"Because my parents gave me everything I ever wanted, they never made me finish anything. They just kept buying me stuff. They never once said, 'No, we bought you an art studio, so you need to finish a drawing.' They just bought me a telescope when I told them that I wanted to be an astronomer."

I COULD NOT BELIEVE IT!!! Everyone was crying with her and I excused myself to go into the bathroom to break the non-emotional look I had on my face. I remember my parents never bought me an Easy Bake Over or a Big Wheel.

I wanted a pink Big Wheel that had the yellow brake handle that you pulled up, so you could slide to the side as you stopped. I didn't get it.

My mom didn't allow me to get a Geri Curl (thank goodness) and because she thought jellies (little plastic shoes) should be worn with stockings, she took them back to the store because she didn't want to be embarrassed if her kids didn't wear them properly.

Oh yes, the tragedy of my childhood with all the times I was told no when I wanted something. I was also given a firm and stern brief before we went into stores, that I better not ask for anything. I started babysitting when I was 12 years old and had 8 jobs before I left for college, because I could get what I wanted with my own money.

To hear this young lady spill her guts about a childhood that I dreamed of and blamed her parents for her inability to keep a job amazed me. I realized then, WE ARE ALL NUTS!!

## Parents Do Their Best

Shortly after that, I read Lois Hay's book, *You Can Heal Your Life*, and realized it was not too late to change. She made a powerful statement and it shook me to my core. She said something like, "Your parents did the best they could with what they had and what they knew at the time, so forgive them."

I was feeling some type of way about my childhood and after reading that, it made me view my childhood from the lens of my rational adult mind, and not from the wounded child. I had a great childhood, but it wasn't perfect. What does perfection look like anyway?

Australian Powerful Parenting Coach, Holly Nunan recommends that parents get to know their children's love language and love them like they want to be loved, instead of treating all kids the same.

After reminiscing about our childhoods with my brother, I wondered to myself, if we grew up in the same house. As the youngest, his childhood experience was completely different from mine and we are only one year apart, so we were always together. As the middle kid, in my mind, I felt my parents didn't give me enough attention. Middle kids are always neglected. We don't get the title of being responsible like the oldest kid, and we aren't spoiled like the youngest. I wasn't spoiled, didn't get my Big Wheel and never saw that Easy Bake Oven. Lol!

Coupling the perspective of his childhood and what Holly recommends, I discovered something interesting. My love language is quality time and physical touch. Today, my brother's love language is the same, but I think "gifts" was a part of his language as a kid. He was ALWAYS happier than me and my sister with the toys that he got. His happiness would bother me, and I can still vividly remember the Christmas he got six Transformer Dinosaurs, and how he rolled around on the floor in sheer delight and overwhelming joy. I don't even remember what I got that year, because I was peering at how happy he was...and I wasn't that happy. *Yes, I admit sibling ridiculousness to make a great point.*

Looking back on my childhood, my mom was a workaholic, so I got that trait honestly. She and my father were always working and we didn't get to spend a lot of time with them (in my mind at least). We were babysat by my aunts and spent time with my grandfather on his farm on the weekends. We were well loved, but I don't remember spending a lot of time with my mom, so there was a void there that I carried for a long time. She never knew and will be stunned when she reads this.

It wasn't a woe is me story of "I never see my mom," but we didn't have a close connection and I was a Daddy's girl. I was a tomboy and wore boy clothes for a long time. I was in essence a dude. A highly attractive dude, who was unaware she was attractive. Ahhh yeah....even cute women are dysfunctional. Lol!

When I viewed this scenario from my adult perspective a few years ago, I saw a different story. My parents were 23 and 24 with 3 children, a house and 2 cars. They were the true middle class that no longer exists. We always had food, shelter and clothing and never lacked what we needed. I may not have gotten everything I wanted, but I always had everything I needed. I'm still not sure why I didn't get the Easy Bake Oven, but after asking my father about the Big Wheel, he said that I was a tomboy and he didn't want me to have it.

How could my brother and I have identical childhoods and totally different experiences? How could I not feel adequately loved by my mom, when she worked hard to ensure our family was taken care of? Our parents really do the best they can, with what they have at the time and at the end of the day, we are all nuts because of them.

What childhood trauma are you holding on to? What didn't you get growing up that you still remember vividly? Did you have a physical or verbally abusive parent? If so, can you trace that back to their childhood? Can you forgive them for it and then ultimately forgive yourself?

I can honestly say that I got my work ethic from my mom, and my creativity and entrepreneurship drive from my dad. As an adult, I'm grateful that I didn't get everything I wanted, because it gave me the determination to get it on my own. We are all who we are today because of our childhoods, but we don't have to be victims of them as adults unless we choose to be. What are you choosing and who do you need to forgive?

I've been around a multitude of families of different races, cultures, socioeconomic and education levels, and I have yet to see a *normal* family. What is normal anyway and who created the measurement for it?

Today, it's so easy to look into the lives of others on television, in magazines or social media and somehow measure our normal by impossible standards. However, reality television has touted dysfunctional as a new level of normal, and sending messages to children that families should be loud and disrespectful to each other, and that's simply not true.

We can always point to our older family members and see their dysfunctions, but can you also look at them and see the good? Can you find the good within yourself and then match it with the good in your family member? Can you then wear that as a badge of honor instead of wearing the dysfunction as a badge of shame and a generational curse?

As you continue to move through this book and let go of some of your baggage and undesired friends, and take control of your life, I really want to you to revisit the story of your childhood and find the other perspective. It's waiting for you if you're willing to take ownership of how you will direct your future. In some cases, your destiny will require you to revisit your past and resolve past pains.

## Family Who Hold Each Other Hostage

Unfortunately, there are some family members that may hold you back from pursuing your goals or destiny. I don't think they do this out of malice, but in an effort to protect you. When we choose to leave the nest and step into unknown territory, sometimes family want to be there to illuminate the path. However, if they haven't walked it, they may deter you from walking it too.

As one of the first people in my family to go to college, there was some negativity and fear spoken. When I was on a ship chasing drug runners in the Caribbean and as I began to develop and gain notoriety in my career, I was met with a multitude of questions and comments like, "Make sure you keep your head down."
"Don't let your head get too big."
"Make sure you keep your feet on the ground."

A lot of first generation college students have this challenge. Our families are used to giving us advice and protecting us, but at a certain point, we exceed what they've been exposed to, and because of that, sometimes their insight and advice may no longer be a good fit for us. It's not that their insight isn't valid, but it's based on what they've been exposed to.

Imagine you were in a 70 story building in New York City. If your family has only ascended to the 5th floor and you've ascended to the 50th floor, what you see and are exposed to will be completely different from them. From the fifth floor, their view may be the brick wall of the adjacent building. They can hear the noise from the streets and the beeping of the trash collectors. They may be able to see and hear loud people from the busy streets and this is how they are gauging their perspective.

From the 50th floor, with the ability to have a 365-degree view, you can see the sprawling city and different boroughs. You can see the Hudson River, the Empire State Building and the Statue of Liberty. You can also see Central Park and some of the most magnificent sun rises and sun sets.

You don't hear the chatter from the street. You aren't awakened by honking horns and beeping trash trucks. Life is a bit different from the top and isn't as busy. It's more serene, peaceful, expansive and the possibilities are endless.

Again, this doesn't make one view better than another, because some people actually prefer different levels. However, if they are offering you insight of what it's like to live your life and they haven't experienced higher levels, can you thrive with their advice?

Earlier this year, while on the porch with several of my older family members, my younger cousin announced that she was moving from our small town to Los Angeles to pursue her dream of being an actress. I thought to myself, "Uh oh...I hope she isn't looking for support for this dream."

Then, it began. "Los Angeles!? Don't they have gangs there?"

"California? Don't they always have earthquakes?"

"Don't you know a huge earthquake is going to come and California is going to crumble into the ocean?"

"Oh no! I could never go there. I would be too afraid for my life."

I just shook my head and laughed to myself, because I knew they weren't meaning to squash her dreams, they just didn't know how to support her. They were looking at her dream with a brick wall in front of them, and she had gotten a glimpse of what life could be like looking above that wall and wanted to explore further.

When they calmed down and moved on to the next subject, I touched her arm and whispered, "Don't listen to the dream killers. It's going to be okay."

Then before leaving, I gave her a big hug and said, "I'm so proud of you. Go and don't come back until you have achieved your dream, even if you have to wait tables like Mariah Carey. It will happen if you don't quit."

A HUGE leap, absolutely yes, but I also know that relentless dreamers can achieve their goals if they never give up. People have to be able to believe in themselves and the impossible in order to accomplish anything and many times their dreams are shot down by well-meaning family members.

Without understanding this, there are rifts and resentment created in families. It may be simply a misunderstanding of perspectives, but for older family members, it can be translated as disrespect or no longer being significant. For others, it can feel like suppression, non-support and the "crabs in a bucket" mentality.

For the most part, family want what's best for us, but they also want to protect us. But protection can also feel like suppression and lack of support. Is your family hindering your growth? Can you relate to the different perspectives and not take it personal, but also know that you may not be able to take their advice anymore? Are you a parent holding your kids hostage to a brighter future because of your limited vision?

**Broken Family Ties**

Is your bond with your family as strong as you would like it to be? Whose fault is it and what can you do to strengthen it? Do you even want it to be stronger?

As we grow and expand into adulthood, the childhood bonds of our family become strained and broken. It's especially difficult for people who left the safety of the family nest and went to explore greater territory. Again, first generation college students have this challenge. When you leave your hometown and expand, you are sometimes subjected to the same treatment discussed in the previous chapter (people being afraid of you leaving them in order to grow).

When I became a part of my former organization and started traveling the world, we didn't have a lot of common stories to share and the strain became greater. Each year away from my small hometown was challenging, because I had less in common with my family as I returned home.

As I continued to assimilate into the majority culture, I started to judge my family against the new standards I had become accustomed to. Nothing was good enough and they REALLY didn't like that. As my stress continued to grow, so did my impatience and there was a wedge so big between us, that I would actually sleep for a few days before visiting them for the holidays.

I was lonely and missed them, but there was some visible and invisible tension and I didn't know how to get back in the inner circle. I felt like an outsider when I was with them. Almost like they were all in the house around a cozy fire and I was standing outside shivering in the cold and rain.

This of course, is all a figment of my imagination, and as senile as it sounds, what story are you telling yourself about your family? Do you have the same connection as you once did, and if not, do you want it back? If so, you need to visit the narrative that's playing in your head in an effort to fix what's broken.

My biggest revelation came as I moved back closer to home nearly three years ago. I was an hour away from my hometown and went to visit my family once or twice a week. They were ecstatic that I was closer to home and wanted to spend time with me. In some part, I felt like they were strangers and actually felt closer to my military friends and their children, than I did with my own family.

But, I wanted to get the connection back. Everyone was getting older and I didn't want to have regrets if they passed away. I wanted to spend time with my aunts and uncles while they were lively and liked to crack jokes, play cards and dance on the sidewalk, rather than visit them in a nursing home and pat their hands.

I wanted to be around my family while they were alive and in order to do so, I needed to figure out how to strengthen the bond. But first, I had to figure out how it got broken in the first place. My mom is 1 of 14 and my dad is 1 of 7, so my family is huge! This was going to be a lot of work, but was worth it, because at the end of the day, family will be there for you, no matter what. At least, this is the case with my family.

## Reacting To Dysfunctional Family

By no longer being in hustle and bustle of DC and not having a stressful career, I was able to clear some head smoke. It's like a veil of clouds lifted off my eyes and my life, and I felt like I had lived a significant number of years in a fog.

When I went to Thanksgiving dinner with my family, I was able to see them in a way I had not seen in a long time. I said, "Wow!! I have not seen *these people* in 14 years!"

If I had come home four to eight times a year over my career, who had I seen then? It was usually people who commented on my weight, my hair, or my clothes. They asked when was I getting married or when I planned on having a baby. You know, all the annoying, stinging questions that family ask. They eventually stopped asking, but the pain from the questions still ran through my body.

It's similar to being bit by a snake. The venom slowly eats away at your skin and vital organs. Depending on the type of snake, the death could be sudden or over time. Carrying pain from the comments or judgment from family was a slow venom corrosion of my soul…and patience.

By the time life, work, and relationships got finished whooping up on me, family just added to the mix. After seeing them with a clearer perspective, I realized they had not changed. *I did*. Both ways, good and bad. Carrying the venom and getting whooped by life created tension and a cloud of smoke. By letting all that go, forgiving others and making a commitment to restore the connection, I actually saw them for who they were.

The secret was embracing them for their "alleged" dysfunctions and loving them anyway. We all have distinct dysfunctions that make up a pool of diversified dysfunctions. What creates a separation of family is judging and labeling people for their dysfunction and not just seeing it as what makes them unique and loving them for it. I called it "alleged" because it depends on who's judging, which will determine the validity of it.

Once I started to remove the negative label from my family member's characteristics, it eased the tension between us. They didn't change AT ALL, what changed was my perspective.

For example: My brother is habitually late. I'm not talking about 10 – 15 minutes late, it's more like 4 hours. It drives me NUTS! I mean, what is he doing with his time? This is who he is and his tardiness caused me to become irate. The longer I remained in my career where timeliness was critical and expected, the more irate I became when I came home to visit.

What's funny with this story is that not only did he not change, but he really doesn't care. At times I was considered high strung, but his personality is completely different. He's laid back and nonchalant. My reactions didn't bother him, nor did they make him show up any sooner. I had headaches, and he was as cool as a cucumber, yet we still eventually made it to where we were going.

One day, we were headed out to our family reunion. He paused and said, "You go ahead. I'm going to wash and dry my white clothes before I leave."

"WHAT???!!!! You are going to do laundry and show up two hours late, rather than leave now and show up on time?" As my stress level lessened, I learned how to control my reactions to other people and their "perceived ridiculousness," so I didn't say anything. I just thought it, and then laughed out loud.

I never knew what he was doing when he was epically late to events. I kind of wanted to know what would make a person casually show up two hours late, but who knew he would decide to do a load of laundry right before walking out of the door? Lol!

Which is more ridiculous – Him doing laundry and showing up late or me continuously getting mad for over 20 years about him showing up late?

Do you have someone in your family that habitually does the same thing over and over again and you continually react negatively to it? Which family member sets you off the most? Do you have a family member that will take a story, twist it and create havoc among several other family members when they retell the story? How many years has this been going on?

Is it more shocking that this person still does this after 50 years, or is the reaction of the people over the 50-year period shocking? I really want you to take note here and recognize that we can't change people. We can only change our reaction to them and the moment we are able to step back and see how we continually react to the same scenario year after year, we can choose a different reaction.

Changing your reaction will lessen your stress and frustration, and will ease the tension between you and others, strengthening the bond. Let's face it, we are all going to die one day. When someone is gone, whether slowly or suddenly, there is no room for shoulda, woulda, coulda. We have to cherish each moment we have here and cherish our family. Will you choose to dissolve the petty arguments and disputes with your family over their normal behavior? Can you release them from your judgment and love them?

## Our Contributions To Dysfunction

As you start to monitor yourself, your reactions and face yourself in the mirror, you'll be able to see how you contribute to the dysfunction of the family. I hate to be the bearer of bad news, but just as much as your family gets on your nerves, you do something to ping theirs too. What is it? How are you contributing to the ongoing rifts in your family?

If you really want to strengthen broken and strained relationships, then working to identify *your dysfunction* is imperative. It will set you free. Now…it will shock you, but after you get over the shock, you can work to make amends.

After being closer to home, I wanted to not only strengthen the bond with my parents, siblings, aunts and uncles, but my cousins as well. I have over 40 first cousins on my mom's side of the family alone, so it's a lot of us. We grew up closely and were tight knit. As time has passed, they were still tight and I became the knit.

Nearly eight months after moving closer to home, my sister posted on social media that she and 5 of my female cousins were at a sports bar 15 minutes away from me. I was greatly disappointed, because they drove 30 minutes to get to it and didn't invite me. I thought to myself, "Don't they know I intend to strengthen our broken bonds?" Actually, they didn't, because I didn't announce it. It was a secret and apparently I was the only one having an issue with the it.

I wrote on her post and asked why they didn't tell me, and she said they made the decision at the last minute. That was a lie and I knew it! My family doesn't do anything last minute, so I was a bit peeved. I had just washed my hair, so I wasn't in a position to go and meet them. My cousin told me that they were going to get together monthly and would call me the following month. I agreed and dropped it.

The next month, my sister posted a picture on social media with her and now 10 of my cousins, all dressed up, and at my favorite restaurant that was 30 minutes past where I lived. Not only did they not tell me, but they passed me to go there. Ohhh, I was HOT! I left a dirty comment on the picture and one of my cousins immediately called me. She said, "I told your sister not to post the picture because you would see it." *Really?*

I could hear them laughing in the background and my pride was hurt. She urged me to come and join them. I said, "No thanks!" and hung up. She called my brother and explained it to him and he sat the phone in front of me. She continued to urge me to come and said that they would wait for me. I didn't say anything, because I didn't have anything nice to say and I was working on controlling my reactions.

I figured they wanted me to walk into the restaurant and set it off, because I wasn't invited. However, I had invested a lot of time and money into creating Christy 2.0, so I wasn't interested in my former behavior. I wasn't mad, but my feelings were hurt. Why didn't they want to be around me and why was I a pariah? I didn't know what to do, and I surely wasn't going to show up to hang out with them, so I just went to bed early.

When I woke up the next morning, I cried for nearly 10 minutes. *Yep, I'm admitting to 3rd grade behavior in an effort to teach. There is a lesson here!*

After getting out my emotional pain of feeling excluded by my family, I decided to do a self-assessment. By that time, I was accustomed to taking ownership of every result I had in my life, good and bad, so I knew there was something *I did* to create this scenario. Now…what was it? How far did I have to dig into my soul to figure out what I was doing to create the same scenario twice? I didn't have to dig far.

I said to myself, "Okay Christy…what did *you do* to make them not want to be around you. Weeeeelllllll…

1. When Sherry told you that she was pregnant right after she graduated from college, you told her that you would tell her congratulations when you were sincere about it and at that moment, you weren't, so you would get back to her.

2. When Janet told you that she was pregnant, you counted on your fingers and determined that she was 27, had a Master's degree and a great job, but only after the evaluation did you say "Congratulations."

3.  When they told you about their shenanigans after leaving the sports bar the previous month, you didn't laugh. They told you how much fun they had and what they were doing at the club afterwards, and you didn't crack a smile.
4.  If they are at the restaurant having drinks and wanted to be loud, you would not approve of their behavior and would give them a dry look until they calmed down and acted like you thought they should act, which is similar to you and your friends.

Then it hit me, "OMG!! I'm a party pooper!! Who wants to go somewhere with someone who judges them and won't let them be themselves? Who wants to hang out with someone who doesn't consider their shenanigans funny? Who wants to be around someone who imposes their impossibly high standards on them and judge them if they don't comply. NO ONE!!"

*Oh yes dear reader, I was a piece of work.*

Being held to high standards because of my leadership position at work and having a security clearance for most of my career, made me hypersensitive to how I could be perceived at any moment. I couldn't afford for someone to **ever** catch me in a potentially compromising situation and take a picture. Nonetheless, a video of me acting in a way that could be taken out of context. One picture, in one moment of time, could be disastrous for my career, so I ensured that I was a square at all times in public. Most of my friends were the same way, so that was our normal, but to my family, that made me a prude.

My family aren't outrageous in their behavior, they just aren't squares. I was indeed a party pooper and they didn't want to be around me, because without me they would have a better time. I busted out laughing and relieved myself of the pain I felt, because *I caused it.* Knowing this, and realizing what I had done, I had some apologizing to do.

As one of the first people in the family to surpass the six-figure mark, I expected for my younger cousins to follow suit. I thought that they should be making six -figures and have certain things in place before starting a family. Since they didn't have those things, I was disappointed when they told me they were pregnant.

HOWEVER, I made six-figures, was stressed out, unhappy and didn't have any kids, because I was a workaholic. I was imposing my standards on them, and my standards didn't really look too hot, and because of that, I hurt them with the comments I made over the years.

Over the next few weeks, I went to my cousins (who had already delivered the babies by then) and we had an adult conversation. I apologized for my judgment and criticism of them and explained that what I expected of them was unfair. I also acknowledged how I didn't make the six-figure level appealing to them with the high levels of stress and aggressiveness I displayed over the years.

They understood, we hugged and now all is merry in Family Land. From that breakthrough, I started to look at everything I had done over the years and how I contributed to strained relationships in my family. I acknowledged my behavior and apologized.

This practice is tedious and painful, but it has significantly changed the dynamics with my family and has gotten me back to where I wanted to be. It's not easy to see your faults staring at you in the mirror, but to have a harmonious relationship with my family has been priceless. We are now close knit and I'm with them around the fireplace and no longer looking in from the outside.

Everything I do and everything I achieve is to set a greater example for them to follow. What's the point of having it all, if you don't have your family there to celebrate? What's the point of making it in the history books, if you miss out on the most valuable time with your family as they continue to age and pass into the next dimension?

My family never knew that I felt disconnected and didn't know that I worked consciously to restore the connection, but they do recognize that I had come home and we are all good now.

Will you do the same for your family? Do you have the courage and the fortitude to be the bigger person and acknowledge what you've done? Can you afford to waste another precious day of carrying discontent for your family, when you have somehow contributed to it?

Let it be known, I HAVE THE GREATEST FAMILY IN THE WORLD!!!!!

# Small Tweaks – Big Results
# All Families Are Dysfunctional

Realizing that none of us will live forever, and you can't choose your family, do you want to strengthen your family bonds? Are they broken or strained? It only takes one person in a family to become rational and everyone else will fall into place. This is what it will seem like when you become the rational person.

I urge you to take some of the action steps to heart and do them. You deserve to show up for your family and give your best and they deserve your best.

## Action Steps

**1. Who Gets On Your Nerves?** Which of your family members get on your nerves? Take out a piece of paper and write their names down. Please don't try to do this your head. Write down:

    a) Who pushes your buttons?

    b) Which buttons do they push?

    c) What's your reaction?

    d) What's their reaction to your reaction?

You'll find that some members simply like to get a rise out of people. Are you their consistent victim? Is it really them getting on your nerves or are they challenging you in an area that you could improve on and you are hypersensitive to it? It's easy to tell them to mind their business, but some family members feel that you are their business.

Are they motivating you to be better or are they holding you back? If they're motivating or nagging you to become better, is that really considered harassment? Well, of course this depends on your perspective, but can you see they are nagging you out of love?

**2. Forgive Your Parents -** Looking back at your childhood, can you realize that your parents did the best they could with what they had? Even if you were abused and think they may have been evil, was there abuse in their past where abuse was considered normal?

Joyce Meyer talks about how her dad sexually abused her for over 15 years and when they were both considerably older, he expressed he really didn't know he was doing anything wrong. If this has happened to you, I recommend you get some assistance with moving from that painful space and into forgiveness.

**3. Season of Separation** – Depending on where you are in life, you may need to separate from certain people in your family if they are always throwing salt in your wounds. This is especially true if you are looking to ascend and go to the next level. There will be family and friends who will speak fearful thoughts to you. Who are those family members?

You don't have to get mad at them and stop talking to them forever, just not at this current time. Can you understand that they may just be wanting to protect you and not take it personal? Regardless, you may need to refrain from sharing your goals and dreams with them. It's hard enough to go after what you want, you don't need more people fueling your fears.

**4. Reconciliation** – Do you have family members that you've lost a connection with and want to get closer? Who are they exactly? Write down their names. Can you even remember what caused the separation or rift? Beside their name, write:

    a) What caused the rift?

    b) Who's taking the blame for it?

        1. 50/50?

        2. All one person's fault?

    c) What was the result?

        1. No longer speaking?

        2. Strained conversation?

    d) What is the worst part about the rift?

    e) There are 3 sides to every story – theirs, yours and the truth:

        1. What is your side of the story?

        2. What's theirs?

        3. Is it a difference in perspectives?

        4. What is the rational and adult version of the story?

5. Honestly….how did you contribute to it?

f) Are you willing to be the bigger person and extend an olive branch?

g) If you viewed the story from another perspective, do you owe them an apology?

h) Even if it's their fault, can you forgive them?

| Action | Date | Notes |
|---|---|---|
| Read | | |
| Understand | | |
| Apply | | |
| See Change | | |
| Pedal to the Medal | | |

Sowing and Reaping

# Chapter 8

# *Sowing and Reaping*

*"Whatever you reap, is what you have sown. If you don't like the crop, you look up whoever planted it. Where do you find who planted your crop? In the mirror."*
*- Jim Rohn*

The Law of Sowing and Reaping is as absolute as the Law of Gravity. Once I learned this concept and started consciously applying it, it changed my life.

When we are unhappy, we tend to focus on and lament over the results. We rarely look at every single factor that contributed to HOW we got the result. We spend most of our time trying to fix, self-medicate or overcome the result, without giving any consideration to the root cause.

For every challenge, problem and undesired circumstance you have in your life, there are contributing factors that got you there. As we've flowed through this book, you should have a pretty good sense of what's going on and the glaring issues you may have in your life. As you start to uncover and resolve the large issues, you should keep digging until you resolve the smaller ones too. The beauty of growth and expansion is, once you start to see and feel the results, you will continue.

If your mind was likened to a garden, what kind of seeds are you planting in it? Are you consciously planting seeds of positivity, spirituality, forgiveness, joy, laughter and happiness? Or are you planting seeds of judgment, hate, shame, guilt and condemnation?

Are you even consciously aware of what you're doing or are you just allowing your thoughts to run amuck? I admit that I didn't consciously monitor what went into my thoughts until I resigned and started hanging around highly personally developed people.

For example, 12 years ago, I used to watch popular talk shows with "Who's my baby daddy?" Then I would watch a show that highlighted and followed people who cheated. While watching these shows, I was planting seeds of distrust, deception, pain, inferiority and a host of other negative seeds. Is it any wonder that I had EXTREME trust issues with men? I was the President of the "Men Ain't Right" Club.

During this time, I met some of the craziest people and had some of the most anomalous dating stories of anyone I knew. My nights would be spent on the phone with various friends recounting the stories of the ludicrous men I was attracting in my life. I could write a book on these stores alone that would have you on the floor laughing. I was so busy focused on the undesired men that came into my life, that I never took the time to see how I contributed to that challenge.

I was planting seeds of beets (I hate beets) and expecting peaches (who doesn't love juicy, delicious peaches?).

Once I learned about the Law of Attraction, took ownership of my results and consciously guarded what I allowed in my mind, I started meeting guys with the traits I desired. I focused on what I wanted and stopped feeding my mind with images and stories of the men I didn't.

What seeds are you planting?

## Overgrown Mind Garden

Have you ever seen the yard of a house that's being foreclosed or the parking lot of an abandoned building? There are a multitude of different types of weeds and some can actually grow to look like trees. Weeds don't need water or sun to thrive, and they are powerful! Weeds can grow through concrete and litter the cracks of sidewalks.

I walk regularly in a new community that's springing up near my neighborhood. They take overgrown fields and bring in large commercial tractors to turn over the dirt and churn it up. They also bring in dirt to make the yard level. After they get finished building the house, a landscaping company shows up with truckloads of sod (grass that's rolled up). They work and unroll the sod on top of the dirt, completely covering it with new grass. They put an extensive amount of water on it to make sure the grass takes root and the pieces of the sod merge and make the yard look like a home. They also plant flowers and water them.

The contractors have to continually water the grass and flowers to make sure they survive and take root in their new dwellings. Once they take root, they have to keep watering them and adding fertilizer to make sure they grow into their optimal appearance.

Without fail, within a few weeks, weeds spring up all over the yard. They make the yard look awful! They crop up around the flowers too. After the houses are sold, people work regularly in their yard to pull the weeds every few weeks to make sure their yards are well maintained. There are others who don't maintain their yards and leave the weeds to take over the grass. I've found a direct correlation in them maintaining their yards and how they feel about themselves. Hmmmm….

With this illustration, the same goes for your mind. Are you even aware of what's growing in your garden or yard? Is it overgrown from neglect? If you aren't sure, how do you feel about your life right now? Do you have contradicting voices running rampant in your head?

Building on the earlier chapters, it's possible to train your mind and set it for positivity, but it's going to take effort. The first step is to assess where you are.

### Current Garden State

Your state of mind is significantly influenced by four things:
1. What you see.
2. What you listen to.
3. Who you talk to/listen to.
4. What you say to yourself.

*What are you watching?* What are your favorite television shows? Are they dramatic reality shows or murder mysteries?

Can you see a direct correlation in your life similar to what I described above with my relationship challenges? Do you have drama in your marriage similar to the people that you watch on television or are you paranoid and afraid when you're in a parking garage because you've seen people attacked in them on murder mysteries?

The paranoid mindset that people have and the violence level in society today can be directly attributed to the number of television shows that show murders, violence, detectives, shootouts and forensic science. I've met a large number of teenagers that want to be forensic scientists and psychologists, because of the murder mystery shows they watch, but won't go far away from home to college, because they and their parents are afraid they will be harmed. I wonder where they got that idea from.

Ten years ago I watched a show that detailed the multitude of ways that young ladies were being killed all over the country. Out of fear for my life, I collected an arsenal of weapons. I was always ready to stun someone with my stun gun, spray them with pepper spray, Taebo them or blow a hole in the wall of my house with the shotgun I bought.

I was paranoid that someone was hiding behind the bushes in front of my house or following me in the mall parking lot. Maybe the car driving behind me for three miles was trying to follow me home and kidnap me, so I kept driving around the neighborhood until I shook them.

I was looking around the corner for danger and ready to defend myself at all times. I was waiting to be attacked. There was no peace or serenity when I walked by myself. It's one thing to be vigilant, it's another to be paranoid. When I realized I was creating my own intense fear, I stopped watching that stuff.

What are the challenges you're experiencing in your life? What are you watching that's contributing to it? If you don't see a direct link, give up your favorite two shows for a month (or television all together) and see how you feel. You're looking for something to be resolved within you and if you are too distracted to figure it out, the best way is to shut down what's creating the negativity. Once you start to feel better and have less squirrels running around in your head, you'll be able to easily identify the challenges that need to be addressed.

Create something new to look at that actually gets you closer to your goals. Create a vision board and put pictures up of things you desire. Want to lose weight? Post a picture on your board of your thinner days. If you don't have one, put a picture of someone who has the body you desire and replace their face with a cut out picture of you. Put the house, car, lifestyle and mate that you desire.

If you want to be happier, put pictures of happy people on your board. Visit it often and imagine yourself with the life you desire and spend less time focusing on how to fix the one that's broken. Remember, molding a new life with clay or piecing together a broken past.

Make two vision boards. One for home and one for work. That way, your goals and dreams will always be in front of you. Also, write your goals and positive quotes on notecards. Carry the cards with you, hang them around your house and desk. I have over 20 3x5" notecards on my bathroom mirror. I have enough space to see myself, the other space is covered with positive quotes. I read them in the morning as I brush my teeth, periodically throughout the day and at night after getting out of the shower and brushing my teeth.

I also have notecards on my computer monitor, the refrigerator, bedroom wall, doors, main television and a few other places. You may think this is a little extreme, but living at a +3 happiness level is also considered extreme, and I'm willing to do whatever it takes to keep the negative voice at bay. You have to retrain and reprogram your mind for positive thoughts. Choose to plant new seeds and keep them fertilized by keeping a vision of what you want in front of you.

***What are you listening to?*** What do you listen to in the first 15 minutes of waking up? The news or talk radio? Screaming kids or dogs barking? What you listen to in the first 15 minutes of your day sets the tone for how your day is going to go.

I used to listen to syndicated radio programs that told raunchy jokes, kept me updated on the latest gossip and news as they ridiculed other people. Sadly, this is considered entertainment and while I was entertained with who got the latest divorce or what tragedy occurred in the news, my mind garden was being overgrown with useless information.

As I became clearer on who I was, where I was going and who I wanted to be, I became very deliberate in what I listened to. Again, clarity is so important, because once you know where you are going, you will know what will and will not get you there.

My success coach suggested that I listened to and watch short videos of Napoleon Hill as I started my day. I didn't take his advice for the first two weeks, and he knew it, because my mindset had not changed. It was reflected in our conversations and he could see that I had not shifted out of my negative state. He had the results I desired (peace, joy, enlightenment), but I had to be willing to surrender my ego and listen.

I had to get uncomfortable and create new habits to get the results I desired. When I finally *applied* the information he suggested, I noticed a considerable difference in my mood on the fifth day. What I was doing wasn't working, so I had to do something different.

I wasn't as cranky and distracted during the day and didn't start on a low scale. As I continued to monitor what I was feeding my mindset with during the day, I slowly overturned the dirt in the mind field, planted new flowers and extended the practice to keep the weeds at bay.

I've learned that you can either feed your new seeds with positive information or you will continue to feed the weeds with negativity. You have to work to cultivate what you desire. One of them has to starve to death. Which one is it going to be for you?

As you think about weeds, remember they have roots too. They will take some work to pull and if you don't continue to work and monitor your thoughts, they will come back.

In some cases, people are resistant to change. Having a new sense of happiness makes them feel uncomfortable. They have been unhappy and miserable for so long, that happiness causes them pain. I work with them to overturn their fields and plant new seeds of happiness and joy, but when they feel their identity is attached to their weeds, they lose a sense of who they are.

It's scary to actually be happy and have nothing to complain about. Over time, those who are not committed to continually doing the work to keep their mind fields well maintained, fall back into apathy and become overrun with weeds again and disappear.

Are you ready to change your life? Because if you are, it's going to take WORK! I promise you that the work will be worth it and the payoff will be so immense, you'll wonder why you spent so much time unhappy.

Standing in the place of happiness and joy that I have today, I cringe at the thought that I spent so many years secretly unhappy. It could be considered an absolute waste of my 20's and 30's, but everything that happened in the past has made us who we are today. We can't change the script. We can't change the circumstances. We couldn't have made them love us more.

What we can do now is focus on where we are going. Today creates our tomorrow.

**Who do you talk to and listen to?** We've already covered this in Chapter 5, so I won't go to in depth here, but the people you surround yourself with play a big role in where you are and where you're going. It's time to clean it up!!

**What do you say to yourself?** This is really going to blow your socks off. Are you even conscious of what you say to yourself about yourself? Sometimes we can be the worst critics of ourselves and no one is meaner than the voice that's in your head. Even today, have you said something negative about yourself to yourself or to others?

Comments like, "I'm fat."
"I'm having a bad hair day."
"My butt is too big. My butt is too small."
"My lips are too big. My lips are too small."
"I'm so stupid for letting that happen."
"They are driving me crazy."
"I am so tired of living this way."
"I wish I was smarter."
"I'm sick and feel helpless."

On and on and on. We let our mouths run rampant about ourselves, even if we don't believe it. It's so easy to say bad things about ourselves, and then wonder why our lives suck. It sucks because we said so, and it came into being. You're fat because you said so. Your butt is flat because you said so. You're sick and helpless because you said so. See how this works?

We have learned to be critical of ourselves from what we watch and usually model it from other people. Negative self-talk and judgment can drive us crazy and keep us in a self-made prison hole. Doing this is so normal, that we don't even realize we do it. It's like driving a car down the road with voice commands. Where are you steering the car? Would it take you where you wanted to go or crash and burn within 60 seconds based on what you are saying about yourself? That time has to come to an end.

Everything that comes out of your mouth following "I AM," you are. What would happen if you actually started speaking life into yourself instead of fear, anger and judgment?
"I am healthy."
"I am amazing!"
"I am happy."
"I am grateful."
"I am at my perfect weight."
"My butt is INCREDIBLE!"
"My lips are perfect."
"My body is perfect."
"I am wealthy."

What if? What if you actually started saying nice things about yourself? What if you actually started saying nice things about yourself to yourself in the mirror for five minutes a day. WHOA!! That would be a game changer!!

I remember when I was told to do this by my success coach. I had also heard about it in *The Magic of Believing*, by Claude Bristol. It's called the Mirror Technique.

When I first started doing it, it was hard. That's when I really saw the ugliness of the negative voice in my head. It was loud and ferocious. It also made me very uncomfortable to stare at myself in the mirror. Interestingly enough, I found that although I looked at myself in the mirror every day, I never really *looked at myself*. The me within me. My inner-me. The being behind the flesh. My soul.

As I started talking to my soul, it awakened within me and brought about a sense of peace and harmony. There are two entities fighting within you and the one you feed the most is the one that will dominate your being. It's time for you to start feeding your inner-me, so it can grow, develop and flourish into who you want it to be and who you want to BECOME.

**Cure Yourself Of An Affliction**

This also works if you have a physical illness. Do you solely focus on the pain of the illness and the conditions of it and question, "Why me?" What about changing that energy and start visualizing being healthy?

Nearly 15 years ago I was crippled with arthritis and had a handicap sign for six months. I was 25 years old and had high hopes and aspirations for my life. After a year of crying, suffering and feeling sorry for myself, I determined that being crippled was not my destiny. I also resolved in my mind that I wasn't meant to take the crazy medications they had me on forever.

I hung up a picture of a fit lady that was standing near the Grand Canyon. I imagined that was me, back in shape and looking out over the horizon at my future. I worked to monitor my stress, anger and the food I ate and after a few months, I cured myself. I didn't know about the Law of Attraction at the time, but I knew that feeling sorry for myself didn't work. I tried the opposite; imagining myself healthy and strong. I also prayed to God, even though I didn't really know He existed at the time. He showed up and cured me, so I can't truly take credit for it.

I offer that to you because the power of your condition rests with your tongue and in your mind. What are you imagining and saying to yourself about yourself? Become aware and work to change it. Will you give the mirror technique a try for five minutes a day, three days a week for starters?

### Planting Seeds In Good Ground

There's a common saying, "If you have a problem, help someone solve a similar problem and yours goes away." I've found this to be true.

We have turned into a "me" society, where it's all about us and what have you done for me lately? Who have you served this week? Do you conduct random acts of kindness, hold the door open for others or take a person's shopping cart back into the store for them? It doesn't take much to serve others and the payoff of positive energy that comes back is well worth it.

One caution to note when you are sowing into other people, make sure they are someone worth sowing into. These people have to be worth your time investment and aren't the same people that you have been creating one sided relationships with. Similar to the young lady I described in the earlier chapter. I talked to her for years and she never took my advice, so she's not considered good ground, because she wasn't using the information.

When I do assist others with their challenges, they actually take the advice and implement it, so I'm able to see how they flourish and change. That's my pay off, and they are considered good ground. I give my time to them, not expecting anything from them in return, other than to use the information to grow.

You can also plant seeds where you need a return in your life. When I launched my first book a few years ago, I asked my friends to forward it to their social media network. Nearly 95 percent of them didn't. I was SO MAD! I was mad because they freely forwarded negative articles, political banter and pictures of donkeys. Anything and everything but my book, even after I asked. It was almost like it pained them to do something for me, when I had given so much to them previously.

There were three lessons in that for me:

1. Whose business information was I sharing?
2. My ground conditions changed.
3. Give without expectation.

After getting over my pouting session, I took a minute to ponder. Since I was mad that my friends weren't sharing my information, I had to question whose information I had been sharing. *Well....no one.* So, how could I expect other people to share my business information, if I hadn't been sharing the information of others. How could I expect a harvest if I hadn't planted any seeds of that kind. I immediately started sharing other entrepreneurs' information and highlighted two small business owners in my network daily.

I was still young in my business, and didn't know what I was doing, so it also gave me marketing practice. They were happy that someone shared their information, so that gave me joy.

Secondly, my ground conditions had changed and I needed to change where I was sowing my seeds. As a mentor to a number of people, I was still spending my time with people who were employed and had guaranteed salaries. However, I was an entrepreneur, without a guaranteed salary and needed to get some returns on that side of the fence. With only 24 hours in a day and getting clear on where I was going, again, I knew what wasn't going to get me there.

Continuing to sow seeds and spend time on the phone with people who were not willing to pay me (they were used to free mentorship), I needed to change that. So I started sowing my seeds (time/energy) into other entrepreneurs, because that's the return I needed.

Thirdly, when sowing seeds, it should be done without expectation. Your return in service won't come from those you serve. But, because of the Law, it will come back from somewhere or someone, at some time. You do your part and leave the rest up to the universe (a higher Being). It is always keeping the books.

When I started sharing my friends' information in my network, I got so much joy out of it that I kept doing it and still do it today. I spend 15 minutes a day on social media pumping people up and celebrating their accomplishments. I leave very brief comments, but they like them. Comments like, Yay! Awesome! Amazing!

It doesn't take long, but people are rarely celebrated by their network. Most people love to sympathize with you, but won't celebrate. When my friends launch books, podcasts or videos, I share them with my network. This is usually in alignment with my goals and messaging, so it's not just random information, but I share it and usually leave a message saying that the person is incredible or amazing.

Sow into good ground, without expectation from those that you serve, and know that you will get a return.

# Small Tweaks – Big Results
# Sowing and Reaping

Did you plant a bean in a jar in elementary school? If so, do you remember your excitement when you saw the plant sprouting through the dirt? It's time to break out your farmer's tools and get ready to go to work. This is a very significant step in your process, because you are now taking responsibility for everything that's going on in your life. If you don't like the crops you are producing, it's time to plant new seeds.

It also gives you a chance to see the unfoldment of the life you are creating. As you start to dig up the weeds (getting rid of negative people) and start to plant new seeds (your dreams and desires), you'll wake up renewed and refreshed as you check the progress of your harvest. Keep your eyes on the life you desire and you will be amazed.

## Action Steps

**1. Take An Honest Assessment Of Your Field** – You can't determine where you are going until you honestly look at where you are. We've already discussed family, who we spend our time with and how what we watch and listen to affects our mindset.

All of these things have contributed to the life you are living today. It is absolutely possible to change, but you have to be honest about where you are.

a) What are the negative results that you have in your life right now?

1. What are your weeds?

2. What are your flowers/desired fruit?

b) Is your field overrun from neglect?

c) What negative results are you getting that can be connected to what you are watching and listening to?

1. Paranoid about safety while watching murder mysteries?

2. Life is full of drama and you're watching dramatic reality shows?

**2. What do you want your life to look like?** – If you took a little time to visualize what you wanted your life to look like, you will know what type of fruit you want to produce. By getting clarity on this, you will be more selective of your activities and where you spend your time. You can't get sweet potatoes by planting peanut seeds.

a) What fruit do you want to produce?

b) What new results do you want to create in your life?

c) What activities will get you there?

d) What activities will take you further away?

e) Who has the results you desire that can show you the way?

f) What personal development events can you go to that will assist you?

**3. Establish Good Ground** – Of course when planting new seeds, you need to know what type of ground you have. Is it fertilized soil, all rocks, clay or concrete? You can't plant new seeds and get a new reality if you aren't open to it and don't believe it. You can scatter seeds all over concrete and water it for days, but they won't grow. Weeds, however, will grow through concrete. You have to truly believe and know that you can change and BECOME who you want to be if you are willing to do the work. I am a living testament that it's possible.

It takes 21 days to establish new habits. We are who we are today because of our habits and if we want to change, we have to be willing to get uncomfortable and change in order to create a new normal. In 21 days, you can have solidified some great new habits that can significantly change your life. Give a few or all of these consideration to implement in your life.

a) Listen to something positive within the first 15 minutes of waking up.

b) Turn your commute into time for personal development. Get self-help books to assist you with your greatest challenges. My podcast Look Up Live Up Leadership is also a quick and fantastic option. It is designed for busy professionals.

c) Write down your goals on notecards and hang them in your bathroom mirror, around your home and office.

d) Write down or make nice designs of your favorite quotes and post them around your home or office.

e) Keep positive information in front of you at all times.

f) Be mindful of the negative conversations you have with yourself and others.

| Action | Date | Notes |
|---|---|---|
| Read | | |
| Understand | | |
| Apply | | |
| See Change | | |
| Pedal to the Medal | | |

Go to www.christyrutherford.com/podcast to get the links to my podcast on Itunes and Stitcher (Android).

Get 12 of my favorite quote images at
www.christyrutherford.com/quotes

# Chapter 9

# *Learning To Say No*

*"You must become consciously aware that your future is generated by the choices you are making in every moment in your life."*
*– Deepak Chopra*

Are you a "Yes" person? Do you cringe at the thought of telling someone "No"? Are you often asked to volunteer and say yes, but then perform the tasks begrudgingly? Are you aware of what would make everyone around you happy, but don't have a clue about yourself?

Do you spend your time making sure everyone else is healthy and provided good food to eat, but don't spend the same time or effort ensuring you take care of yourself? Are you the peace maker, always bringing calm to tense situations, yet get battered by the negative voice in your head?

We only have 24 hours in a day and if you are a busy professional, your time is very valuable. When you give your time to something or someone in efforts that are not moving you forward, you are wasting your time.

I purposely put this chapter near the end of the book, because after going through the other chapters and admitting you are unhappy, checking your inner circle, minding your business, really getting clear on where you are and where you're going, and knowing that you control your circumstances, it's time to make yourself a priority.

It's time to give yourself permission to take better care of yourself, so you can serve others better. Take some time and really think about what you want your life to look like. I can't stress this enough, because once you get clear on what you desire and where you want to be, and when you make the DECISION that you are going to get it, you won't put up with B.S.

**To Do or Not To Do**

Are you the dependable person at work, in your community or other places and you always get tagged with extra tasks or people readily volunteer you to do something without asking you first? How does that make you feel? Do you feel honored that people think of you that way or do you feel like you're being used?

People love people that they can depend on to get the job done and that's good until the you start to feel used and unappreciated. It's easy to feel that way, but if you don't step up and start saying no, others will continue to ask and volunteer you.

As you're getting clearer on where you are, where you're going and what you want your life to look like, you'll know what will and won't get you there. Your activities from this point forward should only be aligned with what will get you there. It's time to take the steering wheel back in your life's car and drive it where you want to go, instead of sitting in the backseat pouting because *you are allowing* others drive and direct.

You may not know this, but *you are allowing* them do it. No one can make you do something you don't allow them do to you. If you are constantly being harassed and put down at work, you are allowing that to happen, because of your unwillingness to leave and seek another job where you're actually appreciated and valued. Yes, a hard pill to swallow I know, but you don't have a lot of time left on this earth, so it's time to get to it.

When someone asks or volunteers you to do something, your decision to participate should be based on:

1. How you will feel when you do it.
2. The expected return.

If saying yes will make you feel like you're being used and/or it doesn't contribute to your goals, then say no. If saying yes will bring you great joy and/or it will get you closer to your goals, then say yes.

As discussed in the previous chapter, with the Law of Sowing and Reaping, you reap what you sow. When you sow goodwill and fellowship into others, you expect goodwill to be returned.

However, if you choose to sow into activities that don't bring you happiness, and you feel like you're being used, you won't receive a positive return, because you didn't perform the act with joy.

It's like putting your money into a vending machine and not getting the right snack. *Wouldn't that make you angry?* If you put your money into the machine once and got the wrong snack, salty instead of sweet, would you attempt it again? Maybe. But if you got the wrong snack again, would you put more money in or just take what you got and eat it anyway without being fully satisfied?

If you put your money in the machine and didn't get anything at all, how many times would you continue giving it your money? The same applies with your time.

We get 1440 minutes every single day. If your time was your money, how much are you giving to activities and people that are not bringing you joy and satisfaction. Are you riding down the road throwing money out of the window by listening to your friend or family member complain about their day at work? Is that getting you closer to your goals?

One of my friends was asked to coordinate a wedding for someone. She's highly organized and experienced in coordinating events, but she's also very busy. Not wanting to say no to someone that "desperately needed her help FOR FREE," she said yes. She put together a beautiful event, but was not happy while she was doing it.

The day of the event, she was frazzled (as with most coordinators) and by the end of the night she was exhausted. This would have been all fine and good if there was a benefit to her doing that, whether monetary, joy or satisfaction. But she felt undervalued, overworked and unappreciated. Even if the bride and groom appreciated it, she felt used.

Can she really blame them for using her and working her into exhaustion or should she look in the mirror and know that she could have said no? She created the situation and therefore can't hold others accountable.

**One Sided Friendships**

Having the opportunity to meet new people and make new friends, I was able to compare them to the long term friends I had. As a life coach and giver, I found that I was ALWAYS giving. I was the one who initiated the calls with most of my friends. I was the one coordinating dinners and get togethers. I was the one calling to check-in on them if I felt they needed someone to talk to. I was the one doing all the work.

I'm not faulting them, I just took inventory of the relationships I had with people giving and taking. If I was the only one giving, it's no wonder I felt depleted and empty. If I was the only one offering advice and comfort, it's no wonder I faced a lot of my challenges alone. I was exhausted from digging everyone out of their holes and one day I realized, I was the only one holding a shovel.

Is that their fault or mine? I actually created this scenario because of my own deficiency. *I needed to be needed.* If I was useful in the lives of others, it justified my existence and satiated my desire to assist others. If I was serving others, I was happy. However, not being served by the same number of people left a huge void in my life, that only became apparent when I separated myself from the people I gave all my time to.

Looking at this illustration, this is how I felt when I was having immense challenges at the end of my career. I was so stressed out and I later found out that a number of my "friends" were waiting for me to burnout. I thought I hid it pretty well, but in hindsight, it was glaringly obvious to a number of people including my family.

They weren't the givers, I was. I gave away all of my oxygen to other people, while they had their oxygen tanks in storage. They didn't need theirs, because they had mine. They were sucking the life out of me and I let them. What's interesting about this scenario is when they saw me burning out, they didn't give me my oxygen back, nor offer to give me any of theirs. They kept asking for assistance, because I made them need me.

They watched me meltdown and didn't step in to save me from myself. Again, I'm not mad, I'm just highlighting they didn't reciprocate what I had done for them. I shouldn't have expected that from them. They weren't the person that used brute and frank honesty to get people's attention. That's my gift. ☺

This scenario is absolutely ABSURD! But, it's happening to millions of people around the world. Are you one of them? Are you near death or depleted from giving away your time, advice, energy, heart, love, etc., to others? Can you really be mad at them for doing what you trained them to do? They depend heavily on you because you trained them to do it.

It's time that you break away from the scenario that **you created**. It's possible and although it will cause discomfort for other people, the energy, vitality and refreshing spirit you will get in return is worth it.

## Make Yourself Non-Negotiable

Why do we have such a hard time saying no? What's the problem really? Was this engrained into us as children by schools or societal norms? I don't know exactly where this standard was set, but the day that I decided to start saying no, my whole life changed for the best.

I went to a personal development event and every time someone made a request, we yelled "NO!!" Just saying it brought about great relief. Try it now. Yell "NO!!!" Lol!

Another problem we have with saying no is that we feel we have to have a **reason** to say no. If we don't have a good enough reason to escape the request, we won't say it. Actually, **not wanting to do it** is a good enough reason. If you are wasting your time or money, that's a good reason. If it won't get you closer to your goals and you won't enjoy yourself when you do it, those are great reasons too. I just gave you five good reasons to say no, do you agree with them?

While at an event a few years ago with some friends, one of them asked if I wanted to go to a football game. She bought a ticket for her boyfriend and since he wasn't able to go at the last minute, her money was going to be wasted, unless she could replace him. Since I was in town for a few days, and had an open schedule, she asked if I wanted to go. I looked at her and said, "No."

She and my other friend were apparently waiting for the rest of the answer, but I was done. I turned my head and changed the subject. I wasn't being rude, of course I didn't think so, but the judgment depends on perspective. I didn't want to go because I:

1. Don't watch football.
2. Don't find the games entertaining.
3. Could find something better to do with my time.

4. Could find something better to do with my money.

Even if she would have offered me the ticket for free, my answer would have been the same, because of the other reasons listed. My other friend laughed later at my response and said, "Christy, you said no and you meant that! You didn't say anything else." She laughed again.

Again, I wasn't trying to be rude, but I didn't want to go. How many times have we showed up to save other people from circumstances that they created and then go along with it in order to make them feel good about us? N-O-T A-N-Y-M-O-R-E. Real friends won't take it personal if you don't do something they desire. Some people may consider that selfish, but if you are living in misery and blaming other people for it, what's the negative label for that?

If you are ready to be happy, then you are going to have to take a stand in your life and do what you want to do, without regard for how others feel about it. We have been beat into conformity and most of the people in the world are miserable because of it. Some people are going to be uncomfortable when you break the mold. If you are ready to live the life you truly desire, be prepared to make tough choices. It's time!

## Sacrificing Self For Others

The key to saying no is again wrapped up in the lessons that have already been shared. Are you sacrificing yourself and your happiness for people that aren't doing anything for you in return? Are you spending your time in activities that won't give you the harvest you desire? Are you planting your seeds (making decisions), based on what you expect in return? Are you doing so with positive energy and joy? All of these lessons and actions are connected.

If you aren't going to feel good about giving your time and energy to others and if you are going to complain about it for the next two weeks, what's the problem with saying no? If you will be wounded by it, what's the problem with saying no? It's time to get clear on the life you desire and then start making the tough

DECISIONS that will get you there. If you are the only one making sacrifices and you're miserable, while everyone else is happy, can you really blame them?

I'm going to beat this dead horse until it turns into dust! Every time someone is not living the life they desire, they point out 20 different reasons and a few people and then blame them. Once you have been informed and enlightened on something, you can't go back. You can't go backwards and if you do, you will sink into a deeper pit, so you might as well do the work to move forward.

Recently, I was staying with a friend and she got her house sprayed for a flea infestation. She also had her front yard sprayed. As we stood outside and talked to the chemical guy, I noticed we were standing downwind of the yard and getting exposed to the hazardous chemicals. I mentioned this and the guy said, "I've been doing this for over 20 years, it hasn't killed me yet."

In my former career, my expertise was in dealing with hazardous materials and chemicals, so I was well versed in how our bodies are affected by chemicals long term and short term. I moved and left them standing there. I'm not responsible for them, I'm responsible for me. So instead of standing there talking to them like I didn't know what was going on, or trying to convince them of what was going to happen, I moved.

When we walked in the house later, he was shaking up a can. He said each can was for 2200 square feet and then braggingly said he sprayed 2 whole cans in the house and back patio. I noticed all the windows and doors were closed and the air was off. I told my friend that staying in the house like that was dangerous and we should leave. She said that she had a few things to do and wasn't ready to leave. She also didn't want to open the windows or doors, because she didn't want her pets to get out. I said, "Okay." I quickly left the house and got in the car with the windows rolled up.

A few minutes later, my friend came outside and asked if I would come in the house and help her move some things. I looked at her and said, "Do you understand that your house is a chemical bomb right now?"

"I don't have time for all of that! Are you going to help me or not?" She asked.

"Look…you don't know what I did previously in my career, but I was very good at my job. If you were an employee for a company that I regulated, and they tried to send you in an environment like the way your house is right now, they would be in serious trouble! I would try to get them arrested. Let's go to a café and let your house air out for a few hours and I'll help you then."

"NO! I need this to be done now! Ugggg! Why are you being like that? Are you going to help me or not?!!

After thinking for a few seconds, with a blank stare, I said "No."

She stormed back into the house and I got back in the car. As I sat in the car, I had a conversation with myself. I asked the following questions:

1. Are you willing to go into a known hazardous environment for her, so she won't be mad at you? Because *you can say no.*
2. When you get a headache, will you not get mad at her? Because *you have the power* to prevent the headache.
3. As you sneeze, your eyes burn and your nose runs as you're exposed to those chemicals, will you not be mad at her? Because *you already know* this is going to happen in your body.
4. When you're sick the rest of the night, will you not be mad at her? Because *you already know* you won't feel well.
5. Will you just suck it up, suffer, and lose a few years off your life in order to make her feel good about you? Because with your training, *you already know* this will be a result in the long run.

6. Can you go in there, get a headache, know exactly why it's happening and not say a single word about it, because you don't want her to think you're not supportive of her? Because *you already know* you can't keep your mouth shut when you are doing something you don't want to do.

After pondering these questions for a few minutes, I said aloud, "**Nope! Not gonna happen!**" I was not willing to place myself in a dangerous situation to appease her. She wasn't willing to air the house out for her safety or mine, so I had done what I could do. I'm not solely responsible for the safety of an adult who had been informed of the hazards. I am however, solely responsible for my safety.

A few minutes later, she came outside and got in the car, leaving the door open. We were still downwind and she was now letting the chemicals from the yard in the car. I felt myself getting frustrated. I was starting to feel like a victim and that wasn't going well, because I know that people will only do to you what you allow. There are always two sides of a story and it's usually based on background, experience and perspective.

She didn't get why I was acting that way. She didn't understand, because that was not her area of expertise and the chemical guy told her she would be okay. What good would it have done for me to get mad at her for something that she didn't understand?

If I'm solely responsible for my own safety and well-being, did I have to continue to be exposed to chemicals? Could I make a rational decision and change what was happening without getting mad, tearing her car door off and yelling? Of course! I got out of the car, grabbed a chair from her garage and walked up the street, so I would be upwind from the chemicals. I put the chair down across the street in front of her neighbor's yard, sat down as cool as a cucumber and started reading a magazine.

She was HOT!!

I know what you may be thinking…well, maybe not. But, I want to make this clear to you, *"You are responsible for yourself, how you allow others to treat you and how you allow others to make you feel about yourself."* When you get clear on who you are, where you're going and why you're here, you will start training or retraining people on how they treat you. Once you stop allowing mistreatment in your life, and set standards for how you want to feel, people will either adjust themselves to stay in your life, or they will go away. Either way should be fine with you, and you will be better for it.

I was reasonable when it came to taking accountability for myself and my actions. I may have been considered unreasonable when it came to my friend feeling like I wasn't assisting her. The bottom line is this, if I would have agreed to go in and help her, then I couldn't complain about it. EVER! Nor could I be mad when I got a headache or started feeling sick. I just wasn't willing to sacrifice my health to make someone feel good about me. I wasn't willing to sacrifice my health for a friendship. I was not willing to do it.

Now, this may be considered extreme, but is it really? How many times have you done something for someone and was mad while you did it? How many times have you agreed to do something and then what you predicted would happen, actually happened and you got mad at them because your point had been proven?

The day that you decide to take responsibility and accountability for everything that happens in your life, you will have to make tough decisions. And once the decision has been made with the rational mind, it will be up to you to take action.

Above all else, I desire world peace. World peace starts with inner peace and harmony within ourselves. You sabotage your inner peace when you do something begrudgingly and then have an epic mind battle with yourself later. I desire inner peace and harmony for everyone, because once we stop looking at outside forces and circumstances as the reason for our unhappiness, we can CREATE real change and lasting happiness.

**Living In Authenticity**

When you change, there are going to be some people who won't be happy about it. That's okay. Remember, they may not come to your funeral anyway. People will criticize you and say that you've changed. Well, yes, you have. Thank them and keep growing. You can either stay small by allowing others to manipulate you into conformity or you can shake off the comments and go for what you want. In a world where misery, discontent and unhappiness is normal, become the exception!

When you change, grow and develop, people will say you're being fake. In reality, the role that you've played for others over the years, to the detriment of your personal desires, is what was fake. You are now being who you want to be. You are now stepping into *who you were meant to be* and that is who you are at your core. Have courage and stand in who you are.

One perspective to note is that people who challenge your authenticity may not realize their lack of authenticity. Conforming is taught, expected and 97 percent of people do it. So, what they say may be true from their perspective....or they are just naysayers. Forgive them for not seeing you for who you are and love them for their dysfunction, while knowing no one can make you feel any type of way about yourself but you.

# Small Tweaks – Big Results
# Learning To Say No

If you look at most adults 30 and older, they become more miserable the older they get. Only two percent of retired people I met are actually happy. We find ourselves in a tangled web from compromising our happiness for others. We don't know elated happiness is possible in our adulthood. We sabotage our future by holding onto friendships that no longer serve us and sell our souls for titles, positions and material possessions.

This is your season of taking charge of your life! Saying no to things and people who are no longer serving you makes room for what you truly desire. Start saying no and change the trajectory of your life. Elevate your happiness on the happiness scale as soon as possible!

## Action Steps

**1. Start Saying No** – I'm not sure if there is an easier way to explain this. Just say no to things that you don't really want to do. When you do so, observe the following and take notes:

    a) How did you feel?

    b) Were they a reciprocating friend or one sided?

    c) Would you have done the task begrudgingly?

    d) Did you die?

    e) Did the person die?

    f) How did they feel about it?

        1. If you felt good and they felt bad, how did that make you feel?

    g) Good seed or bad seed?

**2. Fight For The Life You Want** – As you start to take charge of your life, you'll find that people will feel some type of way about it. I saw a quote that said, "We don't lose friends, we just learn who our real friends are." This is so true! As you grow and develop, there are going to be A LOT of people who won't be with you. However, you'll be able to discern who your real friends are versus those who were there to just use you.

Stay strong. Keep your clarity and know that as you grow, the negative energy and negative voices in your head will dissipate.

| Action | Date | Notes |
|---|---|---|
| Read | | |
| Understand | | |
| Apply | | |
| See Change | | |
| Pedal to the Medal | | |

## Chapter 10

# *What You Do Is Not Who You Are*

*"Can I sense my essential Beingness, the I Am in the background of my life at all times? Whatever form it takes, the unconscious drive behind ego is to strengthen the image of who I think I am, the phantom self that came into existence when thought began to take over and obscured the simple yet profound joy of connectedness with Being or God. Illusion will never satisfy you. Only the truth of who you are, if realized, will set you free."*
*- Eckhart Tolle*

There are a lot of fancy titles out there: CEO of...Head of...Chief of...Senior VP of...Captain of... These titles were not attained easily and with hard work, determination and sheer grit, the impossible became possible. A lot of times high achievers trade our personal identity for what we achieved professionally. There are benefits to that, because you need to become the position in your mind first before you achieve it. You have to act like you are the VP of Marketing, before you actually get the position. You have to obtain the qualities, mannerisms and professionalism of a C-Suite professional before you are invited to join.

Most people who don't achieve high levels of success think they will become the person in the position when they get it, but successful people understand you have to become the person first in order to get it.

However, the greatest challenge of finally getting the position, is when we think we are it and lose our identity to it. *It* is the title. *It* gave us access to an office with a window and a mahogany desk. *It* gives us the income to travel extensively and buy the material possessions that we desire. *It* was won after a number of battles, challenges, setbacks and *it* finally became ours.

But, *it* is not who you are. *It* is a title and a position. You are a being, a human being, a spiritual being. You are not a label or a title. The challenge is when you don't know that you are only identifying with your title and not with who you are.

When your identify becomes wrapped up in your professional identity and then something happens to interrupt the title, there will be problems. It can be a change in the job, or you can get laid off or retire. If you haven't taken self-inventory or personal stock of who you are, if a major shift happens, it can rock your world!

*Question* - Are you so caught up in who you have become at your job, that you've lost sight of who you are outside of it?

*The test* – If you are in the upper echelon of your industry, which is an amazing feat to accomplish, what happens when you're outside of your circle? Can you maintain a conversation with others without mentioning your title? Can you have a conversation without feeling a loss in stature if it involves a person in a higher position?

While at networking events in DC, it's common for people to walk up to me, give me their business card and walk off. Other times, upon first meeting someone, they immediately give me their business card, before we even start talking, in an effort to "establish themselves" in the conversation.

Whatever happened to John meeting Marie? Rather than John, VP of Business Development for (insert company), meeting Marie, Chief Marketing Officer for (insert company). Don't get me wrong, business cards have their place, but they can also be dangerous if you get conflicted in who you are versus what you do.

When we become our titles, we lose the identity of who we are at our core. Problems occur if we get demoted or lose our jobs, because our identity is wrapped up in our jobs. This invokes high levels of stress and anxiety and some people fall into depression. Are we still John/Marie, *a rock star performer and high achiever* or have we been reduced to pieces of crap, because we are now John/Marie *unemployed and seeking an immediate position*?

## All Positions Are Temporary

No matter your profession, unless you're an entrepreneur, your job will end one day. Who are you outside of your job? I'm convinced that this is why some executives refuse to retire and work well into their 80's or until their health fails. They don't know who they are outside of their title, so they refuse to leave and fail to live their glory years the way they imagined in their 20's.

While sitting outside at a café in DC, I remember talking to a lady. She was dressed professionally, but didn't have a job. She talked about being a top executive at a Fortune 500 company and was laid off due to restructuring. Although she was dressed professionally, she was one of the saddest people I had ever seen. They had given her a generous separation package, so she didn't have to find immediate employment, but there was something missing for her.

Validation, credibility, respect and all of those intoxicating factors that come with power. Yessss, **POWER** is intoxicating and can get you higher than any drug. Power is addictive and can rot you to your core if you don't know how to manage it. When you are in a power position, being highly respected becomes your normal. When you are in a power position, people kiss your hindparts all day and you no longer expect it, it just happens naturally. People want to appease you and will do whatever it takes to gain your approval.

Ahhhh yess…..it's AMAZING!! However, when you are no longer in that position, your power, validation, credibility and respect crumble and fall through your hands like sand. It can be devastating if you don't know who you are without it.

The lady mentioned earlier was dressed professionally in the sweltering heat to let everyone know she was somebody important. She was *somebody*. Some people may argue that she may have been dressed that way to network and potentially get another job or to feel good about herself. If that was the case, she wouldn't have been as lost in her sense of self or as sad as she was.

She was unaware of the person, her inner-me. She didn't recognize the Catherine that worked hard, excelled, got multiple degrees and worked herself up the ladder to her position. She forgot that Catherine woke up early and stayed late to make sure she performed with excellence. She didn't realize that although she was no longer the VP of Marketing, Catherine was still an incredible woman who had valuable qualities that other companies were looking for. If her conversation with me would have exuded the confidence, grit and openness that she displayed when she had her title, then her power suit would have exhibited more power.

### Identity Crisis

How do I know the look in Catherine's face? How could I interpret her lost look? Well, because I experienced it, and had already grown and moved through that challenge. I was in her exact position and knew the look of pain in her face and demeanor, because I had seen that look in the mirror reflecting back at me four years ago.

In my previous career, my value became wrapped up in my title and accomplishments. Always looking to get to the next level or high award, I worked 60-80 hours a week. While at home, I studied for certifications and exams that would take me to the next level. I was on a mission to prove the haters and naysayers wrong and it came at a cost. When I left my career, professionally I was 100 feet tall, but on the inside, the inner-me was only 4 feet tall.

When I resigned, I became a part of a network marketing company. It was an incredible experience and I got to meet 5 to 15 new people every day. This is how I got my insight on new people not holding you hostage to who you used to be.

However, I didn't know how much respect I got in my career, until it was no longer given. I didn't know how much my title and credibility validated my existence, until I no longer had the title. Better yet, when people didn't understand who I was outside of my industry and circle of influence, I didn't know who I was. I mean…I knew on the surface level, but not to my core; the deep down inner-me. She surrendered to be successful and that proved to be a wrong move.

Faced with not knowing who I was anymore in the world without my title, my self-image and identity crumbled, and ran through my hands like sand. My head cracked open and my face peeled off. I often wondered if I had indeed accomplished all that I thought or whether it was a figment of my imagination. I have enough awards, plaques, trophies and professional paraphernalia to fill a room, but none of that helped me in my identity crisis.

Can a piece of paper make me feel better about myself if no one outside of my circle can interpret it? Can that Tiffany's crystal award make me feel accomplished, if people aren't treating me with the respect and holding me in the high regard that I was accustomed to?

While networking, I found myself in a common conversation with people of different races and gender. Proudly saying that I was a Lieutenant Commander created respect in military circles, but new people kept calling me Sergeant.

They would say, "What do you do?"

"I just left the Coast Guard. I was a Lieutenant Commander, which is a Major equivalent in the other services."

With a look of sympathy on their face, they would say, "Oh… Have you been in combat overseas?"

"I was in the Coast Guard, not the Army."

"Do you have PTSD?"

"No."

Then with a salute, they would say "Thank you for your service Sergeant."

Now with a raised voice and dirty look, I would say, "Didn't I just tell you I was a Lieutenant Commander??"

"Oh...." After a brief pause, they would look me up and down and say, "Well…you must've been in Admin then."

I would internally combust at the notion that I was considered an entry level employee. Didn't they know the power I wielded in my position?? Can't they see my awesomeness?? I would get so mad and respond aggressively saying, "Now you're calling me a *&%#$%@^ file clerk?!! Do you have any idea who I am and what I've accomplished in my career?"

"I knew you had PTSD!" They would walk off laughing at me.

A few people asked if I had been sexually assaulted while I was in the military and I cursed them out too. I didn't know that people only related military leaders to what they saw in movies or how the media portrays veterans as victims. A lot of people felt sorry for me when I told them I served in the military.

I would get highly offended and yell at them saying, "You feel sorry for me? I have four degrees, I made over $100,000 a year, I lived a life of adventure and YOU….you're bored to death working the same lame job for the past 16 years and have the nerve to feel sorry for me. **I feel sorry for YOU!**"

*Oh yes…now you see why I spent $140,000 to become Christy 2.0. I needed help and lots of it.* Lol!

But seriously, this is real a problem, because so many people suffer with an identity crisis after they lose high level positions. Is this you or someone you know? The problem is unless you've had a similar experience, you aren't able to empathize with others who are having the same issue. They are sad and depressed and no one knows how they feel. When the intoxicating feeling of power is lost, they turn to other forms of self-medication (alcohol and/or drugs) to get that feeling back.

I was fortunate to have coaches during that time and I'm not sure what I would have done without them. I certainly wouldn't be here writing about this experience from a higher perspective.

## False Sense Of Security

Using a kite as an analogy, with a good strong wind, a kite rises high in the sky. It defies gravity and the height of the kite depends on the strength of the wind. You are the kite, and the wind it is your career. The kite can fly high in the sky for minutes, sometimes hours, but in reality it's a false sense of security because the wind cannot blow in that direction and at that velocity for 30 years. The wind can dissipate slowly and the kite gently lowers to the ground (retirement) or a counter flow of wind can send the kite crashing to the ground (restructuring/firing).

The wind represents the false sense of self when you become your title. Some people who become their titles sink into depression or commit heinous crimes against themselves and their family when the title no longer exists. Had they known they were still someone of value without the title, their behavior may have been different.

In addition to people not knowing who I was in person, I remember changing my title on a professional social media site to reflect the shift in my career. I panicked when I realized I didn't have a title. I thought, "What will people think or say if I don't have a title? Who am I without a title? Have I become a piece of crap because I don't have a high level title?"

Observing myself in the panic I thought, "Hellooooo, you are still Christy! You are the same awesome and amazing person without a title. I hope you can see through your vanity and ego and believe that."

In an effort to get over myself and quell that panic, I didn't put a title on that site for nearly two years and now I can't remember what all the inner fuss was about.

Over the past four years, I've learned that the gap between what you are and who you are, can be closed with personal development. With only 24 hours in a day, high achievers usually use that time to propel themselves forward professionally. My request is that you use some of that time to develop yourself personally too.

Listening to audiobooks on the way to and from work is a great way to turn your car into a personal development university. My podcasts are also a great option. You'll find that growing personally will allow you to manage yourself better professionally too.

Now, when I'm out networking and people ask, "What do you do?" I usually say, "I harass people" or "I talk a lot." These are usually non-business related conversations, where the person wants to establish precedence. Personal growth has enabled me not to seek value or approval in conversations with others. My approval comes from a higher source. After getting to know each other better a bit, if they ask again, I will tell them I own several businesses aimed at serving others.

It's amazing to just be *who you are* and not *what you are*. I hope this insight sheds light on your potential unconscious behaviors. The feeling that comes with reconnecting with your inner Being and not being your title is liberating!

## Competing With Others

When the identity of a role has taken over your identity, you constantly compare yourself to other people. In general, we are programmed to compare ourselves to others in order to determine our value. Do you get mad at your co-workers for making more money than you?

The problem with that is you aren't taking personal responsibility for where you are and how you can move up. You have settled where you are and the fact that you resent others for your lower position should be unsettling for you.

Speaking to one of my friends, he talked about how everyone in his office made more money than him. He of course was smarter than all of them and somehow felt disenfranchised that they made more money. He was also smarter than his boss and didn't like to take direction from him.

I asked him a few questions and completely dismantled his superiority of everyone in the office.

I asked, "Are you sure you're smarter than them. Academic standards count in while in school, but they don't hold the same weight in the workplace. What credentials do they have that you don't have?"

"They have different life insurance certifications and licenses, and I don't have as many."

"Why do they make more money than you?"

"By them having more credentials, they can do certain jobs that I'm not qualified for."

"I see... Have you asked them exactly which certifications they have and how it adds to their portfolio?"

"No."

"Have you asked them to tell you how you could step up your game and which certifications you could seek that would increase your value to the company and your income?"

"No."

"Do they like you?"

"Everybody likes me!"

"Are you all independent or competing?"

"Independent."

"I see. So they like you, they aren't your competition and you think they would be willing to share this info with you. But, you haven't asked them. Why not?"

.........(silence)

"Instead of asking them, you've been secretly resenting them for years, because you are smarter than them, but you aren't willing to get the credentials in your off time and do the same amount of work as them."

".......Well, since you put it that way."

He and I also talked about moving to another company since he felt devalued there, but he wasn't willing to take the risk. So, if he's not willing to do the work to get extra certifications and he's not willing to switch companies, how is this everyone's fault but his?

How many years are you wasting complaining about what you can do something about? Taking responsibility for who you are and where you are, gives you the clarity to take ACTION to change it. Complaining does nothing and wastes valuable time. Resenting others because they make more money than you is pointless. Feeling superior to others, because of what you bring to the table really reflects how inferior you feel.

Do the work on yourself and you'll discover a whole new perspective, which will completely change your world for the best.

# Small Tweaks – Big Results
# What You Do Is Not Who You Are

Can you relate to the story of connecting your identity with what you do? Do people give you their business cards without prompting? How does that make you feel? Do you give out your business cards to show people who you are...ahem, I mean what you do?

Knowing that this is detrimental to your present and future, are you willing to do the work and reconnect with who you truly are? As you start to unravel some of your challenges, acknowledge your dysfunctions, get clarity on who you are by releasing excess baggage from friends and resolving conflict with your family, this will occur naturally.

## Action Steps

**1. Observe Yourself** – The key to this is being aware that you may have sacrificed your personal identity for your professional one. That may be enough to create change in your behavior and actions. In social settings or at work observe the following:

a) Do you secretly establish precedence when meeting others?

b) Do you feel uncomfortable when you are in a room where people don't recognize you and your importance?

c) Do you feel devalued when someone doesn't address you by your title or respect? *It's one thing to expect respect when it's been well earned and deserved, but do you "feel" devalued when you don't get it.*

d) Do people make you feel differently about yourself?

e) Are you arrogant? Confidence is believing in the inner-strength of yourself. Arrogance is believing that your position gives you strength.

f) Do you remember the high school version of yourself before the title?

    1. Were they better or worse?

**2. Where You Derive Your Value?** – This is another observation of self and inner work. Only by uncritically observing yourself and doing the work in a non-judgmental way, will you get to the root of who you are and live in your truth. Do the work and set yourself free!

a) Do you derive your value from the material possessions you have?

b) When you are driving your nice car, do you look for the approval, admiration and validation of others?

c) Do you post pictures of your expensive luggage, watches or shoes on social media?

d) Do you post pictures of your big house on social media to show "how much snow is coming down"? ....R*ight, when you really just want to show everyone what your house looks like.*

| Action | Date | Notes |
|---|---|---|
| Read | | |
| Understand | | |
| Apply | | |
| See Change | | |
| Pedal to the Medal | | |

# Chapter 11

# *Forgiveness Is For The Forgiver*

*"Bitterness is like cancer. It eats upon the host. It doesn't do anything to the object of its displeasure."*
*- Dr. Maya Angelou*

**FORGIVENESS.** I saved this for the last chapter on purpose. I hope you're still with me. Forgiveness is one of the hardest things you will ever do, but when you do it, it will liberate you quicker than any other act you can perform.

Forgiveness should be a mandatory subject taught in schools, because it's so powerful. As we have moved through this book and hopefully unraveled a few things that have been going on in your life, it's now time to TAKE ACTION with a new perspective.

Looking at some of the stories that have been shared in this book, the majority have been meant to teach and inspire. However, this wouldn't have been possible if I had not forgiven others or myself.

For some reason, we feel like forgiving others relieves them of what they did to us. We feel like it relieves them of the burden they carry for doing us wrong. It's actually the opposite and has absolutely nothing to do with the other person. Forgiveness relieves you of the burden and allows you to drop the excess baggage. They aren't carrying the baggage, and the toxic emotions (hate, anger, guilt, resentment), YOU ARE.

Forgiveness will relieve you of the toxic emotions and baggage. It will give you a peace that surpasses all understanding and get you closer to living the life you desire. The sooner you truly understand and embrace forgiveness, the quicker your life will change for the best.

## Overcoming Past Hurts

A few years ago, while attending a motivational course, the instructor asked for volunteers to sing a song about our lives. Sitting with someone in her early 30s, she jumped up and down, screaming repeatedly, "Pick me...My teacher said I couldn't do it."

Each time she wasn't chosen, she sank back to her seat and sulked. After the forth evolution, she became more and more withdrawn. Since she was in my peer group and I noticed she was stressed from the rejection of the instructor, I asked, "Which teacher said that?"

She said, "My 3rd grade teacher." ☹

At a different training a few months later, a 55-year-old lady told a story of how she was treated after stealing a pencil when she was only 8. In great detail, she recalled what she was wearing, the smell of the classroom, and the humiliation she felt. She started trembling and crying while telling the story, like she had warped back to that very moment 47 years earlier.

Looking at these stories and countless others, people are walking around every day carrying stress and anxiety and sink into depression, because of what someone did to them 20 years ago. There is empathy to be given, but there is also a part of me that wants to shake them and say, *"Why is this an issue now?!! You have carried that bag for 20-50 years and it has stopped you from reaching your full potential. Will you let it go?!!"*

What bags/old wounds are you carrying around that stop you from living the life you want to live? Have you let someone else's opinion of you become your reality? If someone laughed at a lofty goal that you shared with them, did you put your goal on the back burner?

This is serious, because there are countless people who stopped dreaming or stopped trying simply because of the opinion of one person. One person can shatter the dream of a child and it resonates with them all through their life and follows them to the grave. A number of issues that people have in their adult lives started in their childhood. It's time to let it go!

World renowned motivational speaker Les Brown was labeled mentally retarded in elementary school and carried that label all the way through high school. He didn't let that hold him back and now gets paid millions of dollars to tell that story to top executives at Fortune 500 companies.

Because of childhood trauma, Dr. Maya Angelou stopped talking for five years and was called a dumb mute. We know the indelible mark and impact she's made in this world.

One of Dr. Myles Munroe's teachers called him a half-bred monkey, stupid, retarded, and told him his brain was not developed right and he would never learn. Dr. Munroe earned three Bachelor's degrees in 4 years, a Master's in 18 months, has 5 Honorary Doctorate degrees, published 60 books (48 best sellers) and shared his messages in over 132 countries before his untimely death in 2014.

What has someone said to you that adds to the negative story you tell yourself? How does it play a part in the fear you have in going after your dreams? Looking at the leaders just mentioned, they used the pain of their childhoods to fuel their destiny and achieve greatness. The same is possible for you, but it starts with a DECISION to forgive.

## Forgiveness Rituals

Years ago, watching Oprah and reading a multitude of books, I thought forgiveness was a task. I felt like forgiveness was a big deal and it was a full-time job. I would take a piece of paper and write down aaaaaallll the things someone had done to me (usually a guy in a relationship). I would fold up the paper, while chanting something and then tear it in small pieces. After I tore it in small pieces, I would light the paper on fire, while still chanting.

In doing this, the universe, magical Gods and forgiveness fairies would carry away my anger and burdens with the smoke as it rose into the air. *I honestly can't believe I'm telling you this.* Lol!

Forgiveness was a chore. A painful chore, almost worse than a root canal or taking down Christmas decorations. Forgiveness was a burden of my time and I didn't want to do it. Only when it seemed completely unreasonable to hold on to it any longer, did I conduct a ritual and hoped that somehow, something would relieve me of the bitterness I had for someone else.

One time, I wrote down a list of five people that I needed to forgive. I called each of them or saw them in person and announced, "I forgive you." They looked at me like I was crazy, because they rarely remembered the incident that I was referring to. Also, some incidents occurred several years earlier and they thought it was silly of me to be mad for that long.

For one guy in particular, I had to be intoxicated to forgive him. He was a friend that I dated and it didn't go well and I was mad. He was number one on the list of five people and I had been holding the resentment for nearly three years. I knew I would see him at a mutual friend's birthday party and after two martinis, I was ready. I went up to him and said, "I forgive you," with numb lips and slurred speech.

He said, "What?"

"I forgive you." As I stood up taller to project my higher stance of maturity in the matter.

"Nah. Uh uh. I want a sober apology."

"What? You better take this apology and get out of here!"

"Nope! I want you to apologize to me when you're sober, I don't want it like this."

I stormed off.

The problems with this scenario are:

1. He didn't care and had moved on long ago.
2. I thought I needed his approval for me to forgive him.
3. I was hoping he would see my apology as me being the bigger person.
4. I hoped that he would see the error in his ways and how he hurt me.
5. I wanted **him** to apologize.
6. I was actually baiting him to see if he would reciprocate the apology, so my soul could be at rest.

7. I told him that I forgave him, but really just wanted him to acknowledge why I was mad at him for three years.
8. He needed to be sorry for what he had done to me.
9. I was doing him a favor by forgiving him.

This is a totally absurd scenario, but it's so true. Lol! If you can see the absurdity in my scenario, what are you holding on to? Do you feel like forgiveness is a chore? Do you feel like the other person should be sorry for what they did to you and reciprocate an apology after you "announce" you forgive them?

As you move through the practices in this book and get rid of unnecessary people, situations, family drama and seeing that saying no doesn't cause you sudden death, you will feel a lightness in your body and in your spirit. Once you start to unravel the major causes of why you aren't moving forward and see notable results, you will do whatever it takes to feel better and better. This is when forgiveness will play a major part in your life.

## Forgiveness Is For You

Forgiveness has absolutely nothing to do with the other person. They don't need to know (nor do they care) that you are forgiving them. It's a choice that you will have to make in order to live the life that you desire. If holding on to the resentment of your last boss is what's stopping you from moving ahead in your current company, how is that hurting him/her? It's not.

Holding on to that pain makes you a bitter employee, who tells everyone that their old boss is the reason you aren't where you should be in life. You should have a higher position. You should be making more money. You should be living in a bigger house. You should be able to afford your kid's college. You should be driving a better car. You should be able to take your family on more vacations. You should be happier. You should be on top of the world right now and if it wasn't for that demon that destroyed your life, you would be further along.

Is this really true? Does this sound like the soundtrack of your life? It's time to create a new one, because that one isn't worth repeating to yourself or anyone else anymore. *You and only you are the reason you aren't further along.* When you spend your time looking back in your past and having regret and resentment for what someone has done, you aren't looking forward. You can either look forward at your future or backwards at your past. You can't do them both at the same time.

In each moment, you have the ability to choose what you are looking at. When you mention someone or something in your past as the reason why you can't do something today, in that very moment, you are looking in the past…and you aren't looking at your future. IT'S YOUR CHOICE!

Every single moment. Every single second. Every single scenario. Every single feeling. You have the choice to choose which direction you are going to look in. Are you driving your life's car looking through the rear view mirror (past) instead of the windshield (future), and wonder why you are stuck in a ditch?

It takes discipline and focus to only look forward. The past is easy, because it's familiar and comfortable. But it's also closed and dark. You can't go back to change any part of it. The future is hard, because it's unfamiliar and uncomfortable. However, it's open and expansive with an illuminating light. You can make it any and everything you want it to be. It all comes down to a DECISION and the choice to only look forward and don't look back.

What will you choose?

*"True forgiveness is knowing that the past couldn't have been any different."*
*- Oprah*

### Perception Distorted By Past

Are you viewing your present life through a clear lens or are your glasses filthy from the past? A lot of times, we aren't even living in the present moment. We have allowed the past to cloud our judgment of today and depending on the scenario, we get back into the shoes of the person in the past, and then react from that standpoint. We reach back and react from who we used to be and not who we are, and then wonder why we aren't moving forward.

With the young lady in the earlier example, the more she was rejected by the instructor, the more her demeanor deteriorated into a child-like manner. She was no longer standing in the shoes of her present self. She had gone back to that very moment in her childhood, stood in the wounded child's shoes and projected that energy. She had become the wounded child in that moment.

She started pouting and her body language became more dramatic. It was similar to kids that want to let you know that they aren't happy by flailing their arms and making sudden body movements. She wanted the instructor to know that she was unhappy with his decision to choose everyone but her.

Can you relate to what I'm talking about? When someone pushes your buttons, do you warp back to the previous time that this happened and react from that wounded moment? Do you base your reaction on what you did or didn't do in that instance? If someone made you mad previously and you didn't address it the way you wanted to, is the next person an unlikely victim of double trouble? Remember the pinball machine illustration? How many points are you racking up when someone does something to offend you?

After submitting my resignation letter, I had five weeks before I left the office. I was a wreck. One of my colleagues asked me to return my work cell phone. I told him no since I was working feverishly to prepare for my departure. Two weeks later, he asked again and then started threatening to turn the phone off. I explained to him again that I needed the phone since I was working at home and on the weekends. Already stressed out, his constant harassment was not appreciated. He asked again and threatened to take it out of my hands. Unable to hold back any longer, I unleashed on him. He became "fried rice on the Hibachi Grill!" Lol!

One of his young leaders came around the corner and stopped suddenly in his tracks. He was shocked and completely taken aback at the aggression I displayed. He turned around and retreated quickly. I will never forget the look on his face.

Back in my office, I couldn't believe that I allowed my coworker to get me to display that much aggression and be considered unprofessional by a junior leader who held me in high regard. I went to apologize to the junior leader and he said, "Ms. Rutherford, I've never seen you act like that. I didn't know what to do." I could tell that he was disappointed in me, which made me disappointed in myself.

I was embarrassed and apologized. After thinking about it, I discovered that it wasn't my coworker's continuous nagging about the phone that bothered me. It was the fact that every time I left an office after working hard to set new standards, I was treated like crap. He experienced a wrath that had been brewing for nearly 10 years. Instead of seeing that situation for what it was, the stinging pain from past experiences made me launch on him at a force that was unnecessary. He registered a 9,000 on the pinball machine.

That scenario taught me a valuable lesson about the baggage we carry and how it affects our present perspective. Can you see your present clearly if you are looking through the lenses of a filthy past?

**Forgiveness Is Easy**

How long could you carry one book? Two books? Ten books? You may be able to carry one book for an extended period of time without feeling it, but after a while it will become burdensome and you will feel the weight. You may even be able to carry 10 books around for a short period of time, but when you do so, they will become cumbersome and it will be hard to concentrate on what you're doing, because you have 10 books in the way.

The weight of the books is equivalent to the weight that comes with unforgiveness. It is a weight! Do you wake up exhausted and/or drag out of bed in the morning? Are you tired before you even get started with your day and need coffee before you leave the house and multiple cups in the day? Some people have coffee makers beside their beds. They're really in trouble.

Not forgiving people affects your sleep and it also adds a heavy energy to your body that you may have become accustomed to. When people call your past and unwanted desires "baggage," it's because those bags have weight to them.

After going to a personal development camp in Canada and doing a forgiveness ritual with an Indian Chief, (this was serious), I came back home and was astounded how much lighter I felt. It wasn't about my body weight, but a spiritual weight. I popped out of the bed like a daisy and was shocked that I had been waking up with a 500-pound weight on my chest for years, not knowing that it was connected to my past.

I didn't know I had a 500-pound weight on my chest until it wasn't there anymore. That's the importance of monitoring how you feel and tracking what you did and the result of it in a journal. The weight was considered normal and was compensated with extra vitamins, exercise, coffee and chocolate in the afternoon. I was using external things to fuel my body for a spiritual issue.

Since I had forgiveness issues, I fought people in my sleep and often had nightmares. I carried the baggage and burden of what others had done to me and it was reflected in my dreams. Somebody was always getting slapped in the mouth. Lol!! This added to waking up tired, because I didn't get any rest while I was sleeping, since I was wrestling the past, people and scenarios that I couldn't change or alter.

After coming home from that camp and feeling the way I felt, I started to look for bags, scenarios and people to offload. If I lost 500 pounds of spiritual weight in an hour, what else could I get rid of? Who else was I carrying around? Whose business am I in that's creating weight in my life?

That was nearly three years ago and I offloaded everything! Without old issues, the past, or lingering problems, I see my future clearly and manage myself appropriately around other people. I have pleasant dreams and pop out of the bed like a daisy every single day. I drink coffee, not because I need it, but because it's delicious and I love it. But I only have one 8oz cup in the morning, when I used to need several 12 oz cups throughout the day.

Are you willing to let go of the baggage, the scenarios and the people that are stopping you from living the life you desire? It's a simple as CHOOSING your bright and expansive future over a dark and crappy past. It's about driving your life's car looking through your windshield and not the rear view mirror. You can only choose one. Choose not to attach anything that happens to you today with anything that happened before.

Also be mindful of when other people want to drag you back into your past. Don't let them do it! Some people will ask about your past to be nosey and then walk away informed and you walk away broken and feeling like crap. You are responsible for allowing them to make you feel that way. Sometimes when people ask me about my past, I tell them, "I can't remember what I had for breakfast yesterday, nonetheless what you're asking."

That's usually my final answer and we move on to a different subject, or I move on and leave that person where they are.

# Small Tweaks – Big Results
# Forgiveness Is For The Forgiver

When you forgive others, you will set yourself free!! It is so powerful, yet so misunderstood and underutilized. Choose to incorporate forgiveness with the other lessons and set yourself free to live the life that you truly desire. I am so excited for you!

## Action Steps

**1. Baggage Check** – Taking inventory of unforgiveness will let you know where you are today and how much work you need to get done. Forgiveness is as simple as making a decision that your future is worth it. Your inner peace and joy are worth it too. It's a decision, not a chore.

If you were at an airport and TSA inspected your baggage:

    a) How many do you have?

    b) What size are they? (extra large, large, small)

    c) Are they hard shell (issues you're numb to) or soft cloth?

    d) What shape are they? (square, round, unique)

    e) What color are they? (one color, simple, dramatic)

    f) Would your baggage be over the limit?

If they looked inside the bags, what would they find?

    a) Past hurts?

    b) Who?

    c) Lingering issues?

    d) Dirty past?

**2. Clean Out Your Pain Closet** – In addition to taking inventory of the bags you are dragging around with you, what's in your closet? These are huge issues that you pull out on occasion. Are you rambling around in there, when its actually time to close the door and move on? For this, I offer the following:

    a) Make a list of the past hurts you have been carrying around that you want to liberate yourself from.

    b) Forgive the people who offended you in order to free yourself.

c) Choose to drop the easy bags first and then work on the deeper ones.

Change is not an overnight process, but employing new behaviors that become habits will untie you from mental bondage. Give yourself the gift of freedom. IT'S AMAZING!

**3. Let Go Of The Past** – This is easier said than done, but it also starts with a DECISION. In order to do this, you need to become aware of how your past affects your present reality. Can you view that past incident from your adult mind and see that there is another side to the story? Was there a hidden benefit to that scenario you didn't consider. Like Dr. Munroe's teacher calling him all those names made him prove them wrong. He accomplished more that 99 percent of the people in the world, because of that nasty criticism.

Did that judgment and criticism make you fall down or stand taller? If it made you stand taller, can you thank them and forgive them? If it made you fall down, can you pick up your inner child, brush them off, give them a hug and move forward?

The easiest way to assess what past baggage you are carrying is to look at who makes you mad or what do you hate about your job. It's easy to blame the job or your coworkers for your unhappiness, but really everything you dislike about either of them has nothing to do with them. It has everything to do with yourself.

**4. Looking Forward or Backward** – Be mindful of whether or not you are looking at your future or your past. Your past is energy pulling you backwards and your future is energy calling you forward. Which one feels better to you? Which one will you choose in each moment? Become aware of yourself and your mindset and this will become easier. Your life will never be the same

| Action | Date | Notes |
|--------|------|-------|
| Read | | |
| Understand | | |
| Apply | | |
| See Change | | |
| Pedal to the Medal | | |

Check out my e-course, "How to Reduce Anxiety and Boost Your Happiness." It was designed specifically for you to look at the people and the scenarios that set you off. By getting clear on what's setting you off, you can work to resolve the issue within yourself and with others in order to boost your happiness and live with immense inner peace and joy.

Go to www.christyrutherford.com/programs.

# *Closing*

From this moment forward, you and ONLY YOU are responsible for how you allow others to make you feel. **You** are responsible for allowing someone to make you angry. **You** are responsible for allowing someone to make you feel devalued. **You** are responsible for not moving forward in your life, because what happened in your past.

From this moment forward, **you** are responsible for creating a bright, expansive and absolutely amazing future! **You** are responsible for making yourself happy. **You** are responsible for sowing the seeds you want to reap. **You** are responsible for feeding your mind with positive energy and thoughts. **You** are responsible for forgiving yourself and others, so you can accelerate your results. **You** are responsible for saying no if you don't want to do something. **You** are responsible for strengthening the broken and strained bonds in your family, regardless of who caused it. **You** are responsible for your own, personal spiritual journey with the Source of your choice.

Keep me informed of your progress! Send me an e-mail and connect with me on social media.

For my social media links, go to www.follr.me/christyrutherford

Subscribe to and download my podcasts on Itunes and Stitcher (Android). Links can be found at www.christyrutherford.com/podcast

Take a look at my website for other courses, programs and events. www.christyrutherford.com

**To your success, happiness and unlimited joy!!**

# *About The Author*

Christy Rutherford is a Leadership and Success Coach and President of LIVE-UP Leadership, a leadership development and training company that provides success coaching for mid-level and executive level leaders. She assists leaders with lowering their stress, removing unknown obstacles and accelerating their success.

Christy Rutherford served over 16 years as an active duty Coast Guard officer and is the 13th African American woman to achieve the rank of O-5 in the Coast Guard's 245+ year history. Her tours expanded from: drug interdictions on the high seas; emergency response/dispatch to hundreds of major/minor maritime accidents; enforcing federal laws on 100's of oil/hazardous material companies; responding to the needs of the citizens in New Orleans two days after Hurricane Katrina; a Congressional Fellowship with the House of Representatives and lastly a position that benefited from her wide range of experience.

A Harvard Business School attendee in the Program for Leadership Development, Christy also earned a Bachelor of Science in Agricultural Business from South Carolina State University, a Master of Business Administration from Averett University, a Diploma Sous Chef de Patisserie from Alain and Marie Lenotre Culinary Institute, and a Certification in Executive Leadership Coaching from Georgetown University.

Among her many professional accomplishments, her national recognition includes the Coast Guard Dorothy Stratton Leadership Award, Cambridge Who's Who Amongst Executives and Professionals, Career Communications STEM Technology All-Star and the Edward R. Williams Award for Excellence In Diversity.

Made in the USA
San Bernardino, CA
30 September 2016